Agile M&A

Proven Techniques to Close Deals
Faster and Maximize Value

Kison Patel

© 2019, Agile M&A Inc.

This book is copyrighted material. All rights reserved.

It is against the law to make copies of this material without getting specific written permission in advance from Agile M&A. No part of this publication may be reproduced, stored in a retrieval system, or transmitted in any form or by any means, electronic, mechanical, photocopying, recording, or otherwise, without prior written permission of the publisher.

International rights and foreign translations available only through negotiation with Agile M&A Inc.

Printed in the United States of America

ISBN-13: 978-1-7334745-0-4

Agile M&A®

PROVEN TECHNIQUES
TO CLOSE DEALS FASTER AND MAXIMIZE VALUE

A Practitioner's Guide

Kison Patel

Contents

Foreword 7

Introduction 13

Chapter 1: Fundamentals 21
   a. The Case for Agile in M&A
   b. Agile Project Management & Traditional Project Management: Understanding the Difference
   c. Agile: A History
   d. Agile and Traditional: Quantifying the Difference

Chapter 2: What is Agile M&A? 43
   a. Agile M&A: An Outline
   b. Agile M&A Core Principles

Chapter 3: A Universal Framework for M&A 49
   a. The "Game Plan" Approach

Chapter 4: The Agile M&A Process Model 57
   a. Screening, Diligence, and Close
      • Pre-deal Phase: Scouting and Approach
      • Unifying Corporate Development and Integration
      • The Deal Team
      • Play #1: Project Kickoff
      • Play #2: Standup Meeting
      • Play #3: Priority Backlog
      • Play #4: Team Retrospective
   b. Post-merger Integration
      • Play #5: Parallel Planning for Integration
      • The Post-merger Integration Plan
      • Day One
      • Play #6: Integration Kickoff
      • Play #7: Multi-team Standup
      • Play #8: Multi-team Priority Backlog
      • Ending the Integration Process

Chapter 5. Implementation Strategy for Agile M&A 123
   a. Bring in the Experts
   b. Align Teams
   c. Align Tools
   d. Lead from the Top

Conclusion 132

Appendix 133

Foreword

Organizations around the world need not look far into the future to see the tsunami of business disruption heading their way. In fact, this wave of disruption is already beginning to hit, deeply transforming the way companies operate and engage with customers.

This disruption is reverberating through organizations in every industry. We can see examples of this everywhere: in the financial services sector, blockchain and AI are driving profound change; in health services, digital technologies are revolutionizing healthcare delivery systems. The Internet of Things is creating a connected web of products and componentry in the world of manufacturing and beyond. These technologies have the potential to radically alter the way that businesses function, and quickly: what is working today may very well not work tomorrow. In the face of such profound change, you can no longer rely on old strategies.

Executives must contend with this wave of disruption, appearing on the horizon in the form of technological change, shifting customer preferences, and an evolving regulatory landscape. Let's face it: running an organization for competitive and profitable growth has always been a challenge. But how should executives respond and navigate these new complexities? What business and operational changes need to be made, and how can leaders anticipate future customer demands?

This is the existential plight currently facing executives. They have no choice but to confront these challenges and to ask themselves what it means, constantly reevaluating the place of their organizations in an ever-changing business landscape. As executives encounter these advancements in technology and increased market competition, they face an inescapable choice: disrupt yourself, or be disrupted.

To disrupt yourself, you have essentially two options: to transform from the inside, or to acquire the capabilities that you require to fully evolve. The first option carries significant risk, and requires momentous organic change in people, process, and technology. Considerable investment of time and resources is required to assemble a team, create the momentum, and build the internal capabilities necessary to bring about change. Cultural change is challenging to bring about, and resistance to change can hamper its implementation.

Transforming the essential elements of an organization internally and organically is a long, resource-intensive process that carries uncertain results. Therefore, many organizations are looking toward another more appealing option: acquiring the assets they need in order to remain competitive.

What this means is that organizations are using M&A not only to expand on what they are already doing, but to *transform themselves*, so they can thrive and prosper in the long term. This new strategy represents a very different kind of M&A, compared to deals of the past that looked purely for economies of scale and consolidation of costs.

But if organizations are using M&A to achieve different results, then they must also run the M&A *process itself* differently.

FOREWORD

The M&A process must be more responsive to change, more innovative in style, and more streamlined in approach. At its core, the M&A process needs to be *agile*, so that those involved with execution are more adaptive and collaborative, maintaining a perennial focus on value. Unlike more traditional approaches, an Agile approach helps organizations deliver value even when the final destination remains clouded and open to discovery. It's this level of agility and adaptability that fosters the continuous delivery of value, resulting in transformation.

The message is therefore simple: *if M&A is used to transform an organization, the M&A process itself must also be transformed.*

The traditional M&A approach follows a management paradigm that seeks certainty, standardization, and continuity. It pursues a transactional way of thinking and behaving that views M&A as a process that follows a set of industry norms associated with buying or selling a business — go to the market, make a deal, and close it. There is no inherent problem with this approach; in short, this is how transactions work. But if we rely on past playbooks to make decisions about the future, then we start to sow the seeds of failure. The efficacy of these playbooks in the past does not guarantee that they can meet the demands of the present, let alone the future. To put it more bluntly, if M&A is being used to achieve transformational goals — whether in existing operations, products or customer experience — the transactional approach will not deliver transformational results.

What makes the Agile approach so potent is the way it allows practitioners to adapt quickly to new challenges and opportunities, and to develop clarity and accountability. Furthermore, this level of operational discipline offered by Agile creates a powerful environment for innovation and learning.

The time to act is now. Adopting Agile M&A starts at the top, with leaders fully committed to new ways of working. It is about moving from the traditional playbook approach of the past to a new way of working that reflects the way the modern economy functions. Rather than see M&A as disparate teams working through rote pre- and post-deal steps, Agile transforms M&A into a holistic exercise involving one team, one process, working towards one set of goals. Above all, Agile is about a total focus on value.

Agile M&A is not an option — it is a business imperative. To understand why, organizations need to recognize that M&A is an inherently risky endeavor. There are some organizations that achieve consistent success in their dealmaking, with winning investments. Likewise there are organizations who rarely seem to get it right, with one failed deal after another. Then there is the silent majority: those who get it right sometimes, but not often enough — and these are the organizations that experience the gambling odds when they commit to M&A deals. When investing with such significant sums of money, however, the gambling approach must be replaced with a more rational, modern and coherent strategy that better aligns risks with rewards. Casino odds must give way to more acceptable levels of business risk.

Organizations looking to transform through M&A must see this as an urgent challenge. The very survival of organizations is at stake in this new disruptive economy. Agile

FOREWORD

M&A represents that much needed shift from playbooks of the past towards a more animated and enlightened approach that delivers value faster, with fewer headaches and with greater odds for success. Organizations are responding in our age of disruption by using M&A to transform what they do. Quite simply, it's cheaper, better and faster than the organic alternative. However, to be truly successful, the discipline of M&A itself must leave its legacy past and embrace the age of Agile.

— *Toby Tester, Senior Consultant at BTD*

Introduction

I first started working M&A around the turn of the new millennium. This was an exciting time: America was recovering from the dot-com bubble, the economy grew reliably at 4% per year, the entire business sector entered a period of prime deal-making conditions, and M&A finally emerged from under the shadow of the corporate raider era. In 2003, I founded a boutique M&A firm serving Chicago's lower middle market. I ran the firm for five years, participating in dozens of deals during that time. Then, the 2008 recession brought the market to a halt. It was time to change things up.

I started reflecting on the lessons I'd learned advising on deals, and on the many challenges my clients faced during their acquisitions.

M&A is an incredibly complex undertaking; and, as bankers are fond of saying, no two deals are alike. This means that no two deals will face the same obstacles on the path to success — but as I looked back over the many transactions I'd been involved with, both buy- and sell-side, I realize that many of the biggest challenges arise from a common basis: poor process management.

Even at the highest levels of the industry, I observed highly inefficient deals. For example, during diligence, massive amounts of manpower goes toward collating and analyzing complex financial and operational information. Typically, all of this information is stored in confusing spreadsheets and virtual data rooms. Bankers and company employees email these trackers and Excel documents back and forth repeatedly. Poor version control on documents and massive email backlogs cause profound information bottlenecks, leading to wasted labor and long lead times on simple actions.

These efficiency issues ripple through complex networks of dependencies, creating much larger complications downstream — similar to how a single car changing lanes can create traffic problems down a highway. Once diligence is complete, all of this important information — collected at such great expense — is then simply abandoned, and the integration team must start their next project from the ground up.

It was maddening to watch this process unfold, and I wanted to try to find a way to address some of these problems. Ultimately, I honed in on software. It seemed clear to me that many of the procedural problems facing the industry were directly related to a reliance on technology which was long out of date, even in 2008. These are the infamous "legacy systems": clumsy and inefficient technology that companies stick with because they have become so deeply embedded in corporate functions, and would be too expensive to build in-house. I knew that these systems would someday reach a tipping point, when the losses stemming from poor functionality would make replacement unavoidable. Change

INTRODUCTION

was inevitable, and new software would be critical to future successes in the M&A industry.

So I closed my firm, assembled a team, and founded DealRoom. It was a major pivot. I knew nothing about software design and the learning curve was steep, to say the least. But over the last five years, we designed, prototyped, and fielded an excellent product that I am very proud of. DealRoom combines all the features of a strong virtual data room — a centralized and secure location to store and organize sensitive information — with a collection of supporting project management (PM) tools, like interactive request lists and comment threads for important communication.

The goal was to keep everyone working the deal — from bankers to employees on both the buy- and sell-sides — collaborating on a centralized software infrastructure in real time. This ensures that trackers and requests are not buried in emails, eliminates the type of repeat work associated with malaligned spreadsheets, and reduces wait times on work items across the board. Keeping everything together in a centralized system also allows us to leverage use-data to identify potential bottlenecks and stoppages, and to provide a variety of other analytics to our customers.

Developing DealRoom was an adventure in many ways, but the biggest change it brought about in my professional life was completely unforeseen. Working closely with software engineers brought me, for the first time, into contact with the world of "Agile." Although Agile is currently a high-profile concept in the business world, ten years ago it was barely known outside the software development industry. Coming from an M&A background, I had never heard of it — but when I saw Agile techniques in action, I was an instant convert. Agile methodologies encouraged the software teams I worked with to navigate and execute complex projects in fresh, exhilarating ways that were rich with potential. Agile inspired me to look outside of the technology solution I had originally envisioned, and to view the challenges facing the M&A industry in a broader, more interconnected way. I knew, deep down in my gut, that Agile could revolutionize the dealmaking world.

So, I started my journey to adapt Agile techniques for the M&A industry — a journey ultimately culminating in the Agile M&A process model outlined in this book. I developed the process by making hundreds of discovery calls to working M&A professionals — bankers, corporate development scouts, and integration specialists — and identifying their pain points. I talked with them about the process and workflow of their companies, what was working and what needed to change, what challenges they saw facing the industry, and a variety of other issues.

During the course of this research, I discovered that many companies were independently developing in-house techniques and programs reminiscent of Agile, simply because these approaches are so effective. Industry-wide, teams are moving towards Agile principles without realizing it, constantly reinventing the wheel in the quest for ideal project management. I only encountered two companies, however, openly and explicitly referring to their inorganic growth functions as "Agile": Google and Atlassian, which tellingly have two of the most robust and successful corporate

INTRODUCTION

development programs in the industry today.

Part of the problem here is secrecy. Much of the information uncovered during the M&A process is, by necessity, very closely guarded. This emphasis on security is most vital on the front end of deals, when companies are scouting out, approaching, and ultimately closing with suitable targets. Premature disclosures and informational leakages in these stages can lead to failure, unwanted competitive bids, and even litigation.

This drive towards secrecy, however, has permeated other aspects of the industry as well, creating a quasi-paranoid culture where M&A professionals are unwilling to talk about or share important observations, lessons learned, or information on evolving trends. I would like to see this culture change. I would like to see specialists across the M&A field share their expertise and reflections in an open and collaborative atmosphere.

Impetus for this change has to come from somewhere, however. In this respect, I would like to thank Google and Atlassian for their eagerness to discuss their procedures and processes with me, as well as their willingness to let me share those insights in this book. I would like to thank Atlassian in particular for the pioneering work they already do in information sharing. Their "Team Playbook" is an incredible open source information resource aimed at their peers in other companies. It is freely available online at www.atlassian.com/team-playbook.

As more organizations start to value and practice a similar openness, the faster and more thoroughly our industry will improve.

A final thought on Agile itself: today, "Agile" has become another corporate buzzword. Like "synergy," it has become so ubiquitous and semantically diluted that, in many contexts, it is essentially devoid of meaning. And, as with other empty buzzwords, savvy corporate professionals have come to regard "Agile" and its promises with suspicion. A bewildering variety of proprietary "Agile" sub-methodologies have sprung up like weeds over the past few years — and a considerable industry of expensive training and certification programs are springing up with them. The effect has been something of a glutting of the market, and I suspect that many people are getting a little sick of hearing the word Agile.

If you have any of these misgivings, I hope you will shelve them as you read this book. The fact is that when you get past all the noise and chatter surrounding Agile, it becomes increasingly clear that the success of the movement is driven by one primary factor: Agile works.

I hope that you find a great deal of value in this book, and I hope that you find my case for the power of Agile process modeling in the M&A world convincing. Apply it how you like. Build on it. Grow it. It is a blueprint, a map — not a rulebook.

INTRODUCTION

CHAPTER 1

Fundamentals

THE CASE FOR AGILE IN M&A

Corporate mergers & acquisitions (M&A) is one of the most complex, information-dense, and unpredictable processes within the corporate sector. Over half of all deals attempted fail to meet projected value, and many of those which initially succeed are ultimately unable to capture intended synergies, resulting in spin-offs and divestitures down the line. The benefits of M&A far outweigh its risks, however. A successful deal can revolutionize a business overnight, producing the kind of stunning transformation that sends stock prices skyrocketing. So, despite its many risks, M&A is a first-line growth strategy throughout the corporate world, and year-to-year deal volume continues to increase.

As the industry grows, M&A practitioners face new and increasing challenges. Over the past decade, the M&A operating landscape has changed dramatically: With a growing number of deals, surges in transaction size, and increased information density, older project management techniques are rendered largely ineffective and ill-suited for modern M&A. Advancements in cloud-based computing and collaborative tech tools, meanwhile, offer an opportunity for organizations to modernize and develop new procedural approaches that grow in accordance with the impressive rate of the M&A market.

It is not uncommon, for example, for firms to be acquiring multiple companies at a time — and with the development of pipeline management software, successfully conducting and closing multiple deals simultaneously is increasingly possible. This epitomizes the changing landscape of M&A and the important role which technology will continue to play.

The old model of M&A as transaction no longer holds. Now, M&A is increasingly shifting toward a transformational model. Acquisitions are made not for scale, but for capability or scope. Where transactional or scale deals move toward increasing market share through cost synergies, transformational deals accelerate growth, as acquisitions bring in new capabilities with emphasis on efficiency and cost effectiveness. Evolving business environments mean that we must disrupt ourselves, or otherwise be disrupted. If you are not willing to transform and grow by expanding your scope, you run the risk of being acquired by a company that is. You'll quickly find yourself owned by someone else, or losing business.

In response to this changing landscape, we have developed a unique, innovative solution: Agile M&A. The Agile methodology is specifically designed to eliminate many of the risks associated with contemporary mergers & acquisition initiatives. A new model for M&A comes with a new mindset: rather than focus on pre-planned cost synergies, Agile M&A is based on continuously discovering and capturing value. Transformational M&A takes a nuanced approach: acquisitions are not merely about homogenizing culture in the relentless pursuit of scale, but about harmoniously integrating the newly acquired capabilities and people in a way that preserves culture, and ultimately preserves value. The concept was developed with two main premises in mind:

1. **Traditional approaches to project management fail within the context of M&A.** The informational needs are too complex and the environmental factors too unpredictable for orthodox programmatic approaches to succeed.

2. **Many of the major pain points and obstacles present during the M&A process can be identified and overcome** with the right combination of process, tools, training, and project management approach.

When complemented by the right toolset, the Agile M&A approach enables both sellers and buyers to manage the highly unpredictable M&A processes with maximum efficiency and accuracy.

AGILE PROJECT MANAGEMENT & TRADITIONAL PROJECT MANAGEMENT: UNDERSTANDING THE DIFFERENCE

Throughout this book, "Agile" and "traditional" project management methodologies will be discussed at length.

"Agile" and "traditional" do not refer to specific methods or programs, and there is no "approved" set of Agile or traditional techniques. There are no governing bodies administering or owning Agile or traditional as models or processes. In fact, the concept of "traditional" project management appeared only recently, with the emergence of alternative approaches like Agile.

So, the two terms do not refer to specific processes; rather, they describe broad conceptual approaches to managing complex projects. Strategies for identifying ideal operating conditions drive both methodologies. There are numerous PM methods — like Scrum, XP, SAFe, DAD, waterfall, etc. — in use across various industries. Some methods are based on a traditional approach, while others employ Agile thinking, but it is important to understand that no single approach encapsulates either methodology.

Agile can be understood as a set of values that emphasize flexibility, collaboration, adaptability to change, and continuous improvement with each iteration, but the way in which these values manifest and play out varies with each approach.

First, we will review "traditional" approaches to project management. Project management as a formal discipline first appeared in the 1950s. Developed to improve workflow and productivity in extractive industries, traditional PM techniques are most effective in the management of manufacturing, construction, and resource extraction — that is, industries which require sequential and repetitive steps to produce consistent results.

As the administrative duties of productive and extractive

industries expanded in scope and complexity, and the tertiary business sector as a whole grew in size and economic importance, project managers began to apply the same techniques to purely informational corporate projects like M&A. For such projects, the traditional project management approach calls for a rigid hierarchical structure, top-down management, and a workflow relying on functional groups completing work in sequence. Under the traditional approach, project managers and executives align processes and dependencies at a higher strategic level and hand down work items to functional groups, which are largely isolated from each other.

Traditional project management is not especially effective as an approach to information-based industries like M&A. Some aspects of traditional project management — like having a concrete set of steps to follow, and managing cross-team interdependencies — are applicable to M&A, but many other elements, like hard timelines, are not. Traditional techniques are most successful when project goals are static, activities are completed in a well-established sequence, and operational conditions rarely change.

For industries like M&A and tech, which are fluid by nature, these rigid, linear techniques are insufficient. Despite this misalignment, traditional PM worked *well enough* in the M&A domain for many years, and so provided little incentive to radically rethink the approach. Now, however, as M&A and similar industries become increasingly dynamic and information-dense, it is time to reevaluate.

Much of the developed world has moved away from the productive and extractive industries for which traditional

PM was designed, and is now embracing more fluid, unpredictable sectors like service, finance, and tech. Operational conditions are changing as well. For example, businesses processed and stored information on paper for many years, but more recently they have come to rely on electronic documents like spreadsheets.

As with paper documents, however, electronic documents present obvious version control issues. Like paper documents, when changes are made to electronic documents it isn't always clear which version becomes the "master copy." While it is possible to make copies of individual items, any authoritative changes must be made to an agreed upon "master copy," to avoid creating multiple conflicting versions.

Dictionary: *Version control.* Version control is a workflow issue that arises when pre-cloud electronic documents, like Excel spreadsheets or Word files, pass between numerous people via email. As different individuals make changes to the document without communicating with each other, or accidentally open older versions of documents buried in email chains, divergent copies begin to circulate, resulting in miscommunication, confusion, and duplicate work. With critical documents or time-sensitive tasks, poor version control can have especially serious consequences.

Before the advent of cloud-based collaborative documents and chat tools, working in sequence presented the only viable solution to the problem of version control, with each individual or team performing their work before handing the task off downstream. Unfortunately, this workflow model tends to lead to bottlenecks and work delays, especially as tasks are passed between constituencies. In many cases, significant issues arise with *batch work*.

Dictionary: *Batch work.* Batch work — also known as "clumping" — is a workflow inefficiency which occurs when a team or individual completes their portion of a task and then hands it off to the next team or individual in the work sequence, only to see it languish in an inbox or "to do" list. For instance, employee A might complete a request tracker on an Excel sheet, and then email the sheet to employee B, the next pertinent individual in the work sequence. Employee B, however, is bogged down by other work, and does not address the document until the next day. Employee B then hands the spreadsheet off to employee C, and the same situation plays out again. The work is thus completed in small, productive "batches" or "clumps," separated by long periods of unproductive wait time.

This shift in technology and workflow is only one example of a wide range of changes transforming the business landscape at a rapidly accelerating rate since the 1980s. Our world is more connected, markets are larger, and all aspects of business and life more broadly seem to happen at a faster pace. While presenting potential hazards, the progressive globalization of markets and competition also creates many opportunities. Our current environment favors innovative and adaptable companies. It is no wonder the old management strategies, developed for a completely different landscape, are falling short and slowing continued progress. Enter Agile.

Then & Now:

"Way back when (pick your date), senior executives in large companies had a simple goal for themselves and their organizations: stability. Shareholders wanted little more than predictable earnings growth. Because so many markets were either closed or undeveloped, leaders could deliver on those expectations through annual exercises that offered only modest modifications to the strategic plan. Prices stayed in check; people stayed in their jobs; life was good. Market transparency, labor mobility, global capital flows, and instantaneous communications have blown that comfortable scenario to smithereens. In most industries — and in almost all companies, from giants on down — heightened global competition has concentrated management's collective mind on something that, in the past, it happily avoided: change."

—"10 Principles of Change Management," *strategy + business*, John Jones, DeAnne Aguirre, and Matthew Calderone

At its core, Agile is a problem-solving mindset — a way of conceptualizing and responding to constantly changing environments — which values spontaneity, creativity, and swift reaction to novel situations over established procedure, itemization, and static workflow. Agile is adaptive instead of predictive, iterative instead of sequential, and flexible instead of rigid. Agile is a product of today's corporate landscape—just as surely as traditional PM was a product of yesterday's.

> **Expert Opinions, on Uncertainty in M&A:**
> "I think that traditional project management does work, but I think when you're dealing with the more dynamic nature of M&A, where there's a high degree of uncertainty... that's when it starts to break down. But I think Agile is very much a function of uncertainty and I think M&A can be quite uncertain."
> —*Toby Tester, Senior Consultant at BTD*

Agile thinking heavily emphasizes collaboration, cross-functional transparency, and frequent communication. Modern software platforms and tools empower these values. In fact, these tools make Agile project management possible. New technology enables teams to collaborate in real time, solving the problem of batch work and enabling precise version control. An Agile approach allows for many parallel synchronous workflows, which enables project teams to work in small increments, optimizing the completion of individual tasks while minimizing wait times between items.

Agile	Traditional
Adaptive	Predictive
Centralized information, high visibility	Fragmented information, low visibility
Efficient, relevant data capture, superior analytics	Costly, obsolete data capture, inferior analytics
Real-time collaborative workflow	Parallel workflow with periodic alignment

PROCESS FLOW EFFICIENCY COMPARISON: TRADITIONAL VS. AGILE

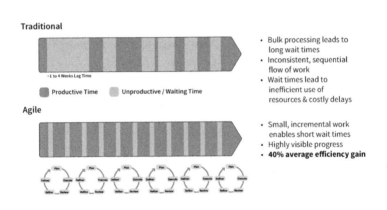

AGILE: A HISTORY

Although the term "Agile" was only formally introduced in 2001, the underlying concepts powering the methodology have existed in various forms since the early 20th century. Beginning in the 1920s, pioneering statistician Walter Shewhart developed a set of techniques now known as the "plan-do-study-act" cycle, which he used to improve processes at the Bell Telephone Company. Shewhart's techniques were championed in the 1950s by W. Edwards Deming, a mathematician and management consultant.

In 1955, Deming gave a series of lectures in Japan in which he advocated the application of statistics to business processes, with the ultimate goal of improving product quality, eliminating waste, addressing bottlenecks and inconsistencies, as well as generally reducing the overall burden of work. Toyota and a range of other Japanese companies quickly adopted his techniques, which ultimately helped to fuel the explosive growth of the Japanese manufacturing industry in the postwar era.

In the 1980s, professors Hirotaka Takeuchi and Ikujiro Nonaka published a series of articles for the Harvard Business Review in which they analyzed the business practices of a number of successful companies, including Toyota, Honda, and Fuji-Xerox. Takeuchi and Nonaka attributed the success of these companies to a combination of speed and flexibility in product development. The business methodology at play found parallels in the game of rugby, which emphasizes teamwork and tactical flexibility in pursuit of victory.

In 1995, software engineer Ken Schwaber and management theorist Jeff Sutherland created Scrum, a software development system named after an element of rugby play. Scrum presented an attempt to extract a workable methodology from Takeuchi and Nonaka's analysis. Scrum has since become the most popular Agile methodology in the world, used to manage both technical and non-technical project work.

In 2001, 17 executives in the software development industry, including Schwaber and Sutherland, met at the Snowbird Ski Resort in Utah to discuss possible innovations in the software field. In particular, the group endeavored to address the limitations inherent in the highly linear, design-based "waterfall" methodology, which was the industry standard at the time. At the end of the retreat, the group released a document entitled *Manifesto for Agile Software Development*, marking the birth of the Agile methodology.

Dictionary: Waterfall Model. The waterfall model is one of the oldest approaches to software design. It is highly linear in nature, with progress flowing sequentially through a series of well-defined stages: conception, initiation, analysis, design, construction, testing, deployment, and maintenance. The waterfall design is an example of a manufacturing-derived "traditional" PM strategy adapted to creative work. Early software designers, seeing the processes that their colleagues in hardware manufacturing used to develop their products, adopted these processes in their own field. The nature of manufacturing means that changes to project parameters can be debilitatingly expensive, necessitating a process model that attempts to anticipate all variables and is extremely resistant to change. Such a rigid framework, however, is not as well-suited to the fluid processes of creative enterprises like software development. Agile thinking embraces flexibility, allowing developers to adapt to changing design needs.

The *Agile Manifesto* outlines a series of four values essential to the Agile approach: (1) **individuals and interactions** over processes and tools; (2) **working software** over comprehensive documentation; (3) **customer collaboration** over contract negotiation; and (4) responding to change over following a plan.

The first value, "**individuals and interactions** over processes and tools," outlines the ideal working conditions of an Agile team. In an Agile operation, people come first. The work environment is collaborative and supports creative thinking. Eschewing older working models based on top-down management and highly linear procedural workflows, Agile thinking favors face-to-face interaction and group problem-solving.

> **Expert Opinions:**
> "Back in 2001, a group of people got together and they laid out a manifesto for better ways to build software. They called it the *Manifesto for Agile Software Development*. The first thing they wrote in their manifesto is that we value individuals and interactions more than we value processes and tools. Processes are good, and of course we need tools, but we value people and people interacting with each other more than anything else. It turns out that when people interact with each other, we get better products and our customers are happier and the build team is happier."
> —*M&A Science Interview with Richard Kasperowski, Author, Consultant and Harvard University instructor*

The second value, **"working software** over comprehensive documentation," declares a preference for quickly fielding workable prototypes or models over completing a comprehensive design upfront. For many years, the standard working model in software design was known as "Big Design Up Front," an approach mandating the completion of a comprehensively documented, fully complete design before coding can begin. This development process contributes to long project lead-times, making it difficult to modify code in response to a customer's changing needs. By prioritizing working prototypes, the Agile approach puts software into the hands of customers quickly, allowing developers to incorporate end-user feedback into subsequent versions, ultimately ensuring that the product grows organically to meet unforeseen needs and achieve optimal functioning.

The third value, "**customer collaboration** over contract negotiation," emphasizes direct and frequent contact with the customer, to ensure that the project adapts to their needs. In traditional negotiations, a software developer typically receives a detailed description of the project requirements from the customer and completes a software design accordingly. The Agile methodology values a more interactive approach, which assumes that designs will evolve over time to accommodate changing conditions.

The fourth value, "**responding to change** over following a plan," encourages adaptivity and flexibility over adherence to a static plan. Traditionally, software developers pursued projects according to highly detailed, predetermined plans with limited flexibility. As a result, developers were inclined to perceive any changes as negative events to be avoided at any cost. By encouraging the development of a project through many iterations, the Agile approach embraces change more effectively.

Following the release of the *Manifesto for Agile Software*

Development, the technology community quickly adopted the four tenets outlined above. The tremendous success of the Agile approach in the technology domain sparked prompt interest in other industries, including biotech, defense, financial services, and marketing. Leading companies in these industries began tailoring Agile processes to address their most pressing project management challenges.

How can one PM technique be so applicable and successful across such varied industries? It is actually pretty simple: Each of these industries face fluctuating priorities, rely heavily on knowledge management, and benefit greatly from effective collaboration. All of these conditions are incredibly well suited for Agile. Agile's flexible nature also allows each industry to implement the specific values that best improve their greatest challenges, making Agile scalable and constructive.

> **Expert Opinions:**
> "If you want to be a more future-oriented M&A professional, you need to take an Agile approach to things… So think transformation, not transaction… It's about leveraging the opportunities from a deal, but to do that you need to take a much more of a transformational mindset, as opposed to a transactional view… When you're thinking about M&A, don't think about continuity, think about opportunity… Don't think about minimizing risk, think about living and breathing risks. Don't look at transaction value, look at transformation value."

— *Toby Tester, Senior Consultant at BTD*

Agile also emphasizes constant improvement towards best practices. Any industry can truly benefit from this approach. An Agile team is never satisfied with a process just because it works, and there is no such thing as good enough. Every working cycle strives to incorporate lessons from completed tasks into future processes, resulting in continuous refinement. Even if a team achieves something resembling a "best practice" in one project, the goals and parameters of their next project will be different — so teams will execute, refine, and continue to improve in accordance with the principles of the Agile methodology.

The original Agile *Manifesto*, penned at Snowbird, is a concise and effective plan for implementation of Agile across many diverse industries. The *Manifesto* presents a broad strategic vision. No highly detailed technical framework will be able to achieve the goal of continuous improvement in every situation.

All of the proprietary, industry-specific Agile methodologies — SAFe, LeSS, DAD, Nexus, etc. — work best in the context for which they were designed. The high-level values of Agile thinking, however, are universal in their applicability, helping companies improve their process flow immensely.

FUNDAMENTALS

AGILE AND TRADITIONAL: QUANTIFYING THE DIFFERENCE

So the Agile approach sounds great on paper. Software development teams swear by it, and there is abundant evidence that it works in other industries, too. But just how effective, ultimately, is a typical Agile process? Can we quantify it? Many have tried, as it turns out.

Between 2010 and 2015, various organizations conducted studies exploring the final outcomes of software development projects following different established project management approaches. A recent survey, conducted by CollabNet for the 13th Annual State of Agile Report (2019), provides additional insights into the current use of Agile project management techniques worldwide.

Based on responses from 1,500 participants across the globe, 97% of surveyed tech organizations currently follow Agile practices in some capacity. And the trend appears to be accelerating: 61% of respondents have been following Agile practices for over three years.

COMPANY EXPERIENCE AND ADOPTION

Company Experience

Source: CollabNet/VersionOne

What is driving this change? The State of Agile Report indicates that organizations adopt Agile practices in pursuit of a number of operational goals, including accelerated delivery, improved adaptability in dynamic operating environments, and increased company productivity overall.

Source: CollabNet/VersionOne

And it is working. Through the adoption of Agile techniques, teams improve their ability to manage change, effectively diagnose and overcome challenges, and more frequently assess a project's state through regular inspection and close collaboration.

Source: CollabNet/VersionOne

If Agile is starting to seem a little too good to be true, it is worth reiterating that context is everything. Agile practices work well in information-driven industries, where creativity and collaborative thinking play central roles. Just as traditional PM strategies fall short in such circumstances, the Agile approach would not make much sense in working environments driven by static, well-established goals. These industries focus on tangible deliverables and generally strive to maximize reproducibility in established, highly linear workflows. Not only would Agile principles not realize any tangible gains in these contexts, but the approach would likely be counterproductive.

In the software development industry, however, Agile produces positive results across the board. The question we are interested in asking is: Would these positive results translate when applying Agile techniques to the M&A process? We will not know for sure until a detailed study appears, but the close similarities between conditions in both industries strongly suggest that what works in software likewise works in M&A. Some companies have already successfully transformed through Agile M&A, in a demonstration of its efficacy and incredible potential. That is to say, we are seeing evidence that it works, even in the absence of a formal study.

Both software development and M&A begin with strong pre-determined final goals, called *True North*: in software development, the goal is usually something like providing the customer with a robust, effective tool carefully tailored to their needs. In M&A, the end goal is more along the lines of effectively incorporating the target acquisition into the existing corporate structure while maximizing value.

Dictionary: *True North*. True North is the guiding principle that drives any project as a whole. It is the highest-level strategic understanding of why a project has been undertaken and what value it is expected to hold for the company. In projects of significant length and complexity (for instance, software design or M&A), challenges sometimes arise when low-level details and tactical considerations cause teams to undertake work or explore avenues that do not directly contribute to realizing the True North objective. Accordingly, it is important for team members even at lower functional levels to periodically widen their vision and consider their work in the context of larger strategic concerns.

The route to achieving these goals varies dramatically from project to project. Just as every software design presents a unique need, so too does every deal and integration project. Teams can rely on previous experience and knowledge, but no linear, itemized blueprint can accommodate the incredible breadth of needs and challenges that emerge during the course of a long and complex project.

The unique advantages of Agile — the way in which it encourages teams to respond quickly and creatively to emerging issues, its ability to foster cross-functional collaboration and visibility across workstreams, and its focus on constantly improving workflow and eliminating waste work — really shine in the types of informationally complex, organically evolving projects typical of both industries.

FUNDAMENTALS

CHAPTER 2

What is Agile M&A?

AGILE M&A: AN OUTLINE

M&A is an information-driven industry, with intense and complex management needs. From the marketing phase through due diligence and post-close integration, maintaining team alignment, facilitating collaboration, and ensuring that the team remains focused on the larger goals presents a considerable challenge. Addressing these long-standing challenges requires an effective and consistent project management methodology. The methodology pursued can have a dramatic impact on how quickly and smoothly a deal progresses.

M&A is in crucial need of such a methodology. Currently, important deal processes are managed with a variety of disconnected tools, which leads to the development of irreconcilable issues with efficiency, organization, and collaboration. Although it may be hard for industry veterans to admit, this system is broken and needs to be amended.

During due diligence, important deal documents are requested in batches through Excel and then dumped into a staging environment. Later, these documents are moved into virtual data rooms where potential buyers can view them. If buyers need additional information that has not yet been answered, they are requested through email or Excel.

This complex and convoluted process isn't only time-consuming but it also creates an opportunity for miscommunication, version-control issues, and breaches in security essential to deal success.

Similarly, post-close integration is often conducted using the same set of tools, relying heavily on Excel and email. Typically, integration teams develop playbooks, which are created using Excel and then distributed to all parties involved in execution for task and goal management. Much like during diligence, this hinders cross-functional communication and collaboration around shared and big-picture goals.

Because Excel does not allow for real-time, centralized engagement, integration teams will often take these playbooks and work through them in their respective functions. This siloed process keeps functional leaders from working together to identify possible roadblocks and execute shared plans to maximize deal value and uncover synergies.

So, no matter which side of the table you are on, it is clear that this workflow has some obvious — and potentially costly — problems. Overall the process is slow, malaligned, and poorly connected, with insufficient communication between functional groups. Lack of version control between spreadsheets leads to duplicate work and time lost trying to hunt down information. Limited collaboration and batching on Excel slows down the overall process immensely, and poor information capture makes it difficult to collect useful data for analytics.

We created the concept of Agile M&A to address such problems. Built on the principles of Agile thinking, Agile M&A provides foundational improvements to how corporations plan and execute complex projects like M&A deals, by building a mindset of collaboration, continuous improvement, and adaptation. The Agile M&A system incorporates lessons from the successful implementation of Agile in other industries to create a model tailored to the specific needs of the M&A industry.

Whether considered from the buy-side or sell-side, the Agile approach is especially well-suited to highly dynamic processes like M&A. In M&A, every deal presents a unique set of needs and challenges. Adopting a traditional, programmatic project management style likely leads to duplicate work, lost information, procedural bottlenecks, and limited cross-functional visibility.

The "game plan" at the heart of the Agile M&A methodology introduces an operating framework to optimize team alignment and collaboration in a way that is modular and flexible, avoiding the issues that arise from a more conventional static "playbook." Approaching M&A with an Agile strategy allows team members to react quickly to emergent deal conditions and for the team to remain cohesive and aligned.

AGILE M&A CORE PRINCIPLES

Building on the foundational work of the 2001 Agile *Manifesto*, the Agile M&A Core Principles are intended to encourage a new way of thinking and working within the M&A world. These principles empower M&A professionals to change the way they collaborate, tackle shifting priorities, and achieve common goals

1. **Individuals and interactions** over processes and tools: M&A projects benefit significantly when people work together consistently to achieve a common goal.
2. **Meaningful progress** over comprehensive documentation: within an M&A project, large volumes of data and materials are created, exchanged, reviewed, and analyzed. The key to a successful M&A process lies in the ability to distinguish between irrelevant noise and the type of critical data that will ensure a deal proceeds on validated assumptions and accurate information.
3. **Real-time collaboration** over sequential work: focusing on direct collaboration is an essential component of a highly-effective Agile M&A team.
4. **Responding to change** over following a plan: a successful Agile M&A team must be able to adapt to changing needs swiftly and fluidly.
5. **Operational transparency** over implicit assumptions: within an M&A project, many critical decisions will be made based on complex considerations. In order to maximize the value of the deal, the M&A team must have a clear understanding of progress, challenges, risks, and obstacles to be addressed.

These five values are the strategic foundation of the entire Agile M&A project. The techniques and strategies outlined in the next sections of this book are built upon the vision defined by these principles — but they are by no means the final word. Any technique or process that aligns with these values has a place in the Agile M&A model. True to the nature of Agile and its principle of continuous improvement, practitioners are encouraged to refine and enrich the strategies and techniques outlined below.

CHAPTER 3

A Universal Framework for M&A

THE "GAME PLAN" APPROACH

One of Agile's most fundamental and defining aspects as a process model is its focus on *iterative workflow*. Following this approach, complex projects are subdivided into small, actionable work-items, which are completed, reviewed, and, if necessary, reiterated, toward realization of the ideal outcome. These work cycles are often called sprints — a concept we will explore later in greater detail.

> **Expert Opinions:**
> "Research has repeatedly demonstrated that short-duration projects are more likely to be successful than prolonged endeavors. Oftentimes business transformation projects involve a mix of complex development efforts, such as business process reengineering, legacy IT system replacement, and the creation of new, innovative business practices that rely heavily

on technology. To increase the probability of project success, structure your project into multiple deployments of small solution components rather than taking the 'big bang' implementation approach. As you develop and deliver the solution in increments, incorporate lessons learned from each increment into the next iteration and constantly test for alignment with business objectives."
— *Kathleen B. Hass, Principal Consultant at Kathleen Hass & Associates, Inc.*

Dictionary: *Sprint.* A sprint is a time-boxed period to complete a set amount of work. In other words, it is the basic unit of iterative workflow — a single pass through a task intended for reiteration. A sprint is one of the building blocks of the entire Agile approach. Sprints work particularly well in software programming, where small parcels of code can be quickly written, executed, debugged, and refined until they reach an optimally functioning end state. Each iterative cycle ends with a potentially shippable product that can be delivered to the customer for feedback.

Sprints help to reveal problems early in the coding process, while maintaining creative momentum, and most significantly, allows for greater flexibility in response to changing project goals or parameters. The same concept can be applied to work items in the M&A process.

See Plays → Fast Learning Cycles

The iterative approach is flexible in its scalability. Iterations can be applied to extremely detailed, low-level items like individual diligence requests, as well as to more high-level, abstract goals, such as integrating HR or aligning value drivers between PMs. Critical to this approach is understanding that any given Agile technique is highly modular. An iterative approach can be used as part of a detailed process model or employed on its own to meet a unique need.

Following this line of thinking, we consider the steps outlined in this chapter as "plays," and conceive our overarching process model as a "game plan." We understand that, within the world of Agile, "plays" can sometimes refer to broad strategic moves (i.e., to the types of acquisitions, like acquihires and so on), but, in the context of this book, "plays" describe a collection of techniques for approaching acquisition. Plays, taken together as a set, comprise a game plan.

Case Files:

The use of the term "game plan," over the more common "playbook," originates with the integration team at the software company Atlassian. After experimenting with traditional playbook-driven approaches to organizing workflow, Atlassian ultimately rejected the playbook, as this model lends itself to the impression that deals and pertinent factors can be templatized. Working experience demonstrated to the Atlassian team that this is a misleading and potentially dangerous impression — and that ultimately no rigid, pre-existing strategy can anticipate the complex needs of an integration project. Atlassian still uses trusted techniques, called "plays," when appropriate, but frame their collection of plays a "game plan" to encourage team members to think beyond the traditional playbook paradigm.

In this chapter, we offer a "process model" which, at the strategic level, enables for the completion of any M&A deal with maximum value-capture. The model consists of two basic game plans: the first covers the front end of the deal — finding a target, completing due diligence, and closing — and the second addresses post-close integration. Taken together, the game plans form a basic framework for approaching any deal confidently and efficiently.

> **Expert Opinions:**
> "Where I have an issue with playbooks is that it becomes this sort of fail-safe that everyone starts to use for any deal going forward. The reality is that each deal — even if it's in the same sector, same geography, same scale — each deal is going to be fundamentally different. And so to expect a playbook to work in a different environment, it almost removes the thinking power and expects some sort of autonomous process to work. I think that's a mistake."
> — *M&A Science Interview with Ben de Haldevang, Founding Partner of Agile Gorilla*

> **Expert Opinions:**
> "You really need to think about development as you go along, and that really is how we approach integration. It's what we found works because in a pre-deal environment you have limited time, very limited information and access to people, and you need to accept that once you get post-deal a lot of the things you assumed are going to be wrong. That ability and that willingness to learn and evolve as you go through integration is that core factor to success."
> —*M&A Science Interview with David Boyd, Founding Partner of Agile Gorilla*

We encourage practitioners, however, not to treat this model as a rigid, linear blueprint for success, but rather as a collection of techniques operating holistically to allow teams to execute deals as effectively as possible. So, teams can follow the process model as a whole, or they can take any of the techniques outlined below to run as plays, fielding plays when appropriate circumstances arise and tailoring the approach to fit operational conditions.

After outlining the process model and its plays, we will discuss a broad range of accessory plays which can be employed to address specific needs or challenges or to increase the efficiency of the game plan as a whole.

> **Expert Opinions:**
> "I'm trying to get people to focus not on playbooks but more on frameworks. What is our stance going to be from the integration point of view? Then, for any given acquisition we will have an OKR [Objectives and Key Results] and OKRs shift pretty regularly and are cross-functional in nature. The actions associated with each of the OKRs go down to pretty impressive depths around all the different areas that need to be touched in order to drive whatever that goal might be."
> —*Chris Hecht, Head of Corporate Development at Atlassian*

The game plan approach aligns well with the rugby metaphors used in the Scrum methodology — and, all things considered, an M&A deal is remarkably like a game of football or rugby. The goal remains the same in each iteration: to win, i.e., to successfully and profitably integrate the target asset. The route to victory is always different, however, as every game unfolds from the same starting point along radically different and unpredictable lines. Only by relying on proven techniques — the plays — and remaining flexible in their application can a team respond to evolving conditions effectively, and achieve victory.

The steps outlined in the next chapter are just that: proven techniques that have helped teams complete complex projects like M&A deals quickly and intelligently.

A UNIVERSAL FRAMEWORK FOR M&A

CHAPTER 4

The Agile M&A Process Model

DEAL FRONT END: SCREENING, DILIGENCE, & CLOSE

The Agile M&A processes outlined in this chapter provide a tactical approach for planning and executing work at ground level, fostering a collaborative, transparent, and constantly improving team dynamics. Agile allows teams to focus their efforts on completing critical tasks in pursuit of a timely and effective closing.

PRE-DEAL PHASE: SCOUTING & APPROACH

A deal does not simply appear out of thin air. A significant amount of work and decision making takes place before a deal approaches the formalized stage of due diligence. Picture an M&A deal as a wedding: before a wedding can take place, the hopeful suitor must find a fitting partner to court. An M&A initiative enters a similar period of courtship, with acquirers seeking out suitable companies with which to merge.

Acquirers develop a business strategy, which defines overall objectives, capability gaps, priorities, and the potential areas in which M&A may be useful. A small and select group of executives and corporate development personnel, maybe working with an investment bank, initiate the M&A process. This group scouts out potential buyers or sellers in accordance with the broad strategic goals driving the intent to purchase or sell — the *acquisition strategy*.

Dictionary: *Acquisition Strategy.* The acquisition strategy is the ultimate goal guiding M&A initiatives, the fundamental strategic objective motivating the desire to buy or sell — the True North towards which everything is oriented. A software company, for instance, may want to expand its product offering in a particular area, or a manufacturing company may want to achieve production synergies in a given geographic region. A company may wish to acquire new intellectual property, human talent, or industrial equipment, or expand its customer base. Acquisition strategy is defined at the highest levels of the company before the search for potential target companies even begins — and it should remain foregrounded throughout the entire M&A lifecycle.

Oftentimes, corporate development professionals discover potential acquisitions as part of ongoing market research. In other instances, investment banks suggest the deal, or otherwise the deal emerges as the brainchild of a company's CEO, product managers, or other top-level executives. Once a target is identified, the corp dev team runs early due diligence, focusing on financials and market assessments. If the corp dev's analysis suggests that the asset is a good fit, the companies will sign a letter of intent (LOI), and the formal M&A project can begin.

For most companies, the M&A process unfolds as follows: the corp dev team completes the confirmatory due diligence phase, the executive team makes the formal decision to close, and the project is then handed off to the integration team to complete. M&A is an explicitly two-phase project conducted by independent teams — and this disjunction sets the integration team up for failure.

Let's return to the marriage analogy. The front end of the deal parallels the courtship period, and the union of two families in marriage can be considered as the merger. As with marriage, M&A is not just about the big wedding day: closing the deal is just the beginning of a life together, of the two parties now acting as one. Both require ongoing work and deep understanding to find long term success and happiness.

UNIFYING CORPORATE DEVELOPMENT AND INTEGRATION

In a 2018 letter to his shareholders, Warren Buffett made the following observation:

"Once a CEO hungers for a deal, he or she will never lack for forecasts that justify the purchase. Subordinates will be cheer*ing, envisioning enlarged domains and the compensation levels that typically increase with corporate size. Investment bankers, smelling huge fees, will be applauding as well. (Don't ask the barber whether you need*

a haircut.) If the historical performance of the target falls short of validating its acquisition, large "synergies" will be forecast. Spreadsheets never disappoint."

This is not a very charitable picture of the motivations driving M&A, but it contains an element of truth nevertheless. High-level executives and corp dev teams are often overly enthusiastic about potential deals.

In certain respects, overexcitement is inevitable. Upper echelon executives are often far removed from the low-level operational details of their companies — and corp dev personnel typically come from investment banking backgrounds, where the deal itself is considered more important than the particulars of its execution. Both groups tend to focus on the high-level strategic potential of target assets, downplaying or ignoring more tactical considerations. When they rally behind a particular deal, their enthusiasm and conviction create a pronounced bias towards positive target assessment.

Integration specialists can provide a counterbalancing perspective, and encourage the team to develop a more realistic and nuanced picture of the asset. All too often, however, these specialists are not consulted during the diligence process.

In these situations, corp dev inevitably sees everything through rose-colored glasses. The team tends to overestimate the value that a target asset will bring to the company, and consequently downplay or outright ignore potential red flags revealed during diligence. Often, the executive-level personnel in charge of finalizing the deal will have unofficially decided to close with the target long before signing the LOI. Corp dev conducts confirmatory due diligence as

THE AGILE M&A PROCESS MODEL

a legal formality, and only truly revelatory discoveries will cause the buyer to walk. Post-close, the new asset is dumped on the integration team, who then must figure out a way to make it valuable.

Case Files:

In 1998, Daimler-Benz (now Daimler AG) announced that it was "merging" with Chrysler in a stock swap valued at over $35 billion. At the time, this was the largest international deal ever. From a strategic perspective, the merger seemed like the perfect match: the two automakers had complementary product offerings, and were expected to achieve significant production synergies by consolidating their manufacturing.

The large synergies forecast by both boards ultimately legitimized the deal in the eyes of the shareholders, who overwhelmingly approved the deal shortly after it was proposed. But less than 10 years later, after suffering massive losses, Daimler spun off Chrysler for only $7.4 billion. What went wrong?

Well, just about everything. The deal was made in bad faith to begin with. Daimler-Benz made a big show out of presenting the deal as a "merger of equals" — guaranteeing brand independence, dual headquarters and boards, the use of English as the standard corporate language, and, of course, the incorporation of "Chrysler" into the new company name. In reality, Daimler-Benz regarded the deal as a takeover. In 2000, DaimlerChrysler CEO Jürgen Schrempp announced to the German paper *Handelsblatt* that Daimler-Benz upper management had always viewed the Chrysler deal as an acquisition, explaining that 'The Merger of Equals' statement was necessary in order to earn the support of Chrysler's workers and the American public, but it was never reality." Schrempp's statement angered many Chrysler employees, who felt that they had been duped by their new partners. The erosion of faith contributed heavily to the poor internal alignment of the two companies — goodwill is one of the most important intangibles driving deal success.

And those forecast manufacturing synergies? Such synergies never materialized. Daimler-Benz originally agreed to share a wide variety of parts with Chrysler, in a move to drive production costs down. Daimler-Benz rolled back this plan considerably, however, ultimately providing Chrysler with very little manufacturing support — support Chrysler desperately needed to remain competitive at a time when Japanese automakers dominated the American market. Ultimately, Daimler-Benz's promise to maintain dual headquarters and boards, coupled with their failure to integrate Chrysler's manufacturing infrastructure into their own, meant that Chrysler was run more or less as a wholly independent subsidiary, failing to realize synergies of any kind.

"You had two companies from different countries with different languages and different styles come together yet there were no synergies. It was simply an exercise in empire-building by Juergen Schrempp," remarked Dave Healy, an analyst with Burnham Securities.

According to George Peterson, another analyst, Schrempp forced the deal through without doing his homework. "Due diligence? Daimler-Benz never did due diligence before it bought Chrysler, never looked into the future to see whether

THE AGILE M&A PROCESS MODEL

Chrysler could afford to be competitive with the others in the industry." Chrysler also rushed into the deal, although for a different reason. In 1998, Chrysler attempted to forestall an imminent hostile takeover by billionaire investor Kirk Kerkorian, leading their CEO Bob Eaton to seek out Daimler-Benz as a white knight alternative. As former Chrysler chairman Lee Iacocca later remarked: "Eaton panicked."

In the end, almost everything went wrong with the DaimlerChrysler deal. Both companies failed to complete the proper upfront research and due diligence. Full integration was never achieved, or even attempted. Bad faith and malaligned company cultures fueled resentment and poor performance. The deal resulted in a disastrous spin-off for Daimler and a second bankruptcy and government bailout for Chrysler, leading many analysts to regard the DaimlerChrysler deal as one of the most catastrophic M&A failures of all time.

Expert Opinions:
"Corp dev people are often investment bankers who are just interested in finding targets to be acquired. It's what they do. Then the integration team is stuck with making the acquisition valuable."
— *Integration Specialist at Autodesk*

"For corp dev, it's all about the deal. That's what they know. [...] Some of the people I've run across are literally like deer in the headlights when they are faced with integration challenges."
— *Integration Specialist at Verizon*

DaimlerChrysler may sound like an extreme example, but this type of failure is unfortunately quite common. Traditional thinking tends to treat the dealmaking and integration phases of the M&A lifecycle as separate projects carried out by independent teams. The disconnectedness of the phases (sometimes referred to as 'The Great Divide') creates a deep rift in communication between corp dev and integration, with potentially serious consequences for both teams and the deal's long-term success.

Approaching the M&A process as a series of discrete projects is a textbook example of a traditional style of project management. The traditional emphasis on linearity and sequential workflow ultimately fails to meet the needs of a complex and dynamic process like M&A.

The first step towards addressing those shortcomings and improving the M&A process is simple: treat the M&A lifecycle as a holistic process. Approaching M&A as an integrated project likely means rethinking how you conceive of M&A at the most fundamental level. Throw out the idea that M&A consists of two distinct projects. The separation between the corp dev and integration teams in a traditional approach to M&A is highly problematic: since corp dev is not accountable for post-close success, their overambitious assumptions can create trouble for the integration team responsible for validating the deal.

Instead of this disjointed and misaligned approach, envision the integration effort as an organic extension of due diligence, with corp dev and integration operating as a close partnership during the entire M&A lifecycle. This synthesis is the essence of Agile M&A: Agile M&A realizes a true partnership between corp dev and integration, or even their functioning as a single team. In practice, bridging the gap between corp dev and integration can be approached in a variety of ways. The specific route taken will vary for each project, depending upon the unique requirements of individual deals and the nature of the companies involved. However, the Agile M&A Process Model advocates a universal governing strategy: to strive to incorporate an integration perspective as early in the M&A lifecycle as possible. Using the integration team to conduct confirmatory due diligence is a particularly effective approach and one which serial acquirers in the tech industry are increasingly beginning to adopt.

Broadly speaking, the Agile M&A Process Model approaches the M&A project as follows: the corp dev team conducts early diligence of potential targets, ideally with the help of the integration lead and relevant functional experts. When corp dev lands on a likely acquisition, the integration team then assembles and begins to consider the post-merger integration plan. The integration lead becomes involved early in the process and is responsible for validating value drivers and delivering on projected synergies. The deal lead's early involvement allows for the development of attainable goals, circumventing conventional issues that arise from overambitious forecasts.

Following LOI, the integration team conducts confirmatory due diligence — the process of identifying risks and ensuring that what is being represented is accurate. Since this team will be responsible for integrating the target, they take this process very seriously. Around this time the Integration Management Office (IMO) should be established as well, if necessary — serial acquirers may be running an IMO continuously. The IMO is deployed to assemble and coordinate small cross-functional teams to complete integration tasks.

> **Expert Opinions:**
> "Having the team that does diligence be a part of the integration is really important because if [the integration team has access to] certain information earlier, [they will do] things differently. During the transaction and diligence, you build really strong relationships with the inbound management and team members. Those relationships are the same ones that are really helpful during integration. I have been on [diligence] teams where we have not engaged in integration until really late in the transaction. I do feel sorry for the deal leads because we have to spend time backing up and understanding why we are at this point in the transaction. I think if you know more earlier and can shape those early conversations, and get the key data sooner, then you will have a better idea of the plan, which ultimately stacks the deck in favor of the acquisition being successful."
> —*James Harris, Principal of Corporate Development Integration at Google*

The consolidation of traditionally distinct teams into a single highly effective unit helps to address two of the largest and most common problems in M&A: overestimating synergies, and inadequately preparing for integration. Since the integration team completes the entire M&A project, they benefit from an inherently more developed understanding of the project, a greater degree of visibility, and superior access to information. This represents a vast improvement over the fragmented relationship traditional corp dev and integration teams employ. The Agile approach to M&A is based upon these advantages. Meanwhile, if the foundation is built upon with the right combination of tools and techniques, the integration team will be able to operate with the speed, flexibility, and teamwork characteristic of Agile's approach.

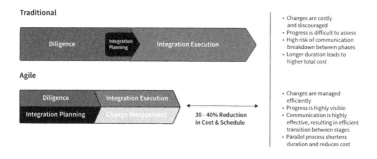

Additional resources for integration planning available at agilema.com

THE DEAL TEAM

In order to clearly differentiate this new type of team from the standard integration teams already in use throughout the industry, we call it the **deal team**.

The exact composition of the deal team depends on a number of factors and will vary from project to project.

Certain figures will always be present, such as legal counsel, tax attorneys, and accountants. Bankers and consultants may also be involved during the diligence phase of the project, as many deals are mediated and/or financed by investment banks, and their involvement should be considered during team configuration. The composition of other team members is contingent on the nature of both the acquiring company and the target company.

A very large serial acquirer often maintains a dedicated corporate development group of up to 30 or 40 members, including functional experts, integration specialists, ex-bankers, lawyers, accountants, and other experienced M&A professionals. Companies of this size often pursue multiple acquisitions at once, and the corporate development group may field multiple deal teams with varying degrees of overlap.

In smaller companies or those which only makes occasional acquisitions, maintaining a large corporate development department is not feasible or economical. More commonly, a dedicated corporate development group of five or fewer members will be assembled as needed. Groups like this depend on a network of internal advisors to provide functional expertise in evaluation of potential assets and tend to rely more on external support figures like consultants and bankers. Both large serial acquirers and smaller organizations can form a successful team without a dedicated corporate development group.

Whether you're configuring a deal team at a large serial acquirer or a smaller organization, the team should include two figures: the **deal lead** and the **deal PM**.

The deal lead owns the M&A process overall, and is

responsible for the end-to-end success of the project. In many cases, the deal lead is someone from the corp dev team, although this is contingent on many variables, including the size of the company and the type of acquisition. The deal lead assists in validating targets pre-LOI.

Upon signing the LOI, the deal lead determines the makeup of the deal team, based upon their understanding of the acquisition and the best path towards its execution. The deal lead plays a critical role in ensuring that the evolving project remains in alignment with the strategic goals driving the M&A initiative as a whole. When integration comes to an end, responsibility falls to the deal lead to close the books.

The deal lead, coordinating with the corp dev team, takes charge of external communications with the target company, the executive team, and other parties over the course of the project, and is responsible for reporting final results post-close. The deal lead assigns roles and responsibilities, authorizes the use of resources, and pulls in outside support as needed. A senior executive often fills this role — they typically possess the necessary combination of strong leadership, strategic vision, and decision-making authority required to succeed.

The deal PM operates directly under the deal lead and is responsible for end-to-end program management. As the official head manager of the deal process, the deal PM encourages teams to operate according to Agile principles and techniques, and provides training and support as necessary.

For a deal PM to succeed, the following attributes are essential:

1. **Experience.** The deal PM should be a certified Agile

project manager, with a proven track record overseeing complex, multifunctional projects.
2. **A love of detail.** The deal PM is responsible for processing complicated and finely detailed information. Negligence, when it comes to details, can have serious consequences.
3. **Broad Expertise.** The deal lead and the deal PM pull it all together. Both must understand every aspect of the M&A process, and see how the different pieces all fit together. This is especially true for the PM: in order to effectively coordinate and support the team on the tactical level, the PM must be a pseudo-expert in every functional area of the project.
4. **Good people skills.** A successful PM marries technical expertise and effective communication, engaging all members of the team.

The size and composition of the deal team will vary, based on the nature of the target asset, the acquisition strategy, and the resource requirements of the M&A project as it evolves. Larger M&A initiatives often involve several teams working in parallel. When this is the case, the deal lead and PM coordinate the different teams. A multi-team project environment often requires additional leadership roles to support intra-team communication. Ideally, each individual team within the multi-team unit will include a team leader or project manager to serve as the coordinator/facilitator.

THE AGILE M&A PROCESS MODEL

TEAM CONFIGURATION OPTIONS FOR AGILE M&A

Option	# of Teams	Total # of Team Members	Process Model	Advantages & Risks
A	1	< 10	Standard Agile M&A	Efficiency will be maximized at 10 people or less, and degrade if total # exceeds limit
B	2 or more	3 to 12 per team (average; customizable)	Scaling techniques for Agile M&A	Additional roles required to ensure adequate communication channels are implemented

Regardless of the deal team configuration, the deal lead and PM employe the same basic techniques — the plays — to establish an Agile workflow.

OPTIMIZING DEAL MANAGEMENT AND EXECUTION THROUGH AGILE M&A AND CUSTOM GAME PLANS

Once the deal team has been assembled, with appropriate skills distributed across various disciplines and departmental functions, the Agile M&A Process Model is ready to be deployed in support of active management of project tasks. Maintaining team alignment throughout the deal is challenging, however, as teams lose sight of the big picture and become consumed by individual tasks. Accordingly, Agile's "game plan" model keeps the team focused on the larger strategic goals of the acquisition.

As a deal progresses from diligence into integration, these challenges become increasingly complex. Integration projects in which large organizations must consolidate assets — such as systems, services, information technology infrastructure, and so on—often consist of intricate activities that affect all functional areas of the business. In many cases, such projects are highly complex, resource-intensive, costly, and disruptive. A poorly managed integration project has the power to diminish the overall value of the merger or acquisition and can compromise the company's revenue-generating capabilities.

Due to the way integration is commonly conducted, industry-wide challenges include communication breakdowns, inefficient use of personnel resources due to delays and unclear priorities, as well as excessive overhead for information management. Executing integration sequentially, following a predictive model, is simply not an optimal strategy in today's highly volatile business domain, where priorities change frequently and adaptability is essential.

In order to meet the industry's highly dynamic needs, we developed the following integration model based on Agile principles.

FULL-SCALE AGILE M&A INTEGRATION MODEL

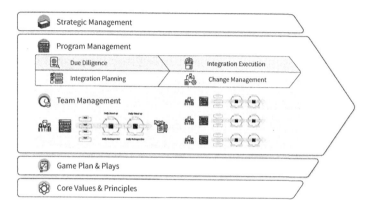

Printable version available at **agilema.com**

Medium-to-large M&A engagements frequently encounter challenges regarding the organizational strategy for utilizing team resources in the most effective way. Some deals are too large and too complex for a single project team to manage. To accommodate this, the Full-Scale Agile M&A Integration Model is specifically tailored to support M&A initiatives involving many project teams. Designed to allow large companies to manage multiple, parallel workstreams simultaneously, this scalable integration model facilitates management of all activities, beginning with due diligence and following all the way through post-close integration.

In short, this model provides corp dev teams with a single framework from which to plan, coordinate, and execute activities across all functional departments, enabling seamless collaboration and the fluid transfer of knowledge across as many as 20 project teams.

The leadership team provides the strategic directives that define the organizational priorities and initiatives of the Agile M&A integration. Their guidance drives program and project teams to collaborate in the planning and execution of projects. The Integration Model provides the framework by which organizations establish a customized game plan composed of individual Agile plays. The game plan model allows several teams to work cohesively to plan and execute initiatives together — this is imperative during the diligence stage, where fragmentation of team resources often leads to the loss of critical domain knowledge is often lost after deal closure.

Leveraging the collaborative nature of the Agile M&A Integration Model, teams begin the knowledge transfer process as a natural extension of executing work in an Agile way; project team members assimilate and spread knowledge across the program organically and efficiently, without incurring additional effort or cost. As a result, this knowledge management approach enables integration planning to begin much earlier in the overall process. Planning and executing work in parallel and utilizing multiple teams optimizes the overall integration process, and increases the quality of the output significantly due to the short feedback loops and rapid learning cycles.

To leverage the power of this model, practitioners implement specific structured yet adaptive activities: customized "game plans," comprised of detailed task management techniques known as "plays." The traditional concept of the "playbook" — a rigid, one-size-fits-all, formulaic approach to managing corporate integration activities — no longer corresponds to today's highly unpredictable M&A world. Managing work in an environment of shifting priorities, and with a high degree of uncertainty, demands a more fluid and dynamic approach.

Concepts like "plays" and "game plan" are designed to provide guidance on specific practices at the level of both team and program. The plays provide a flexible framework from which organizations can build their Agile M&A game plan, which is customized to fit the specific needs, requirements, and context of the initiative.

Imagine it as analogous to a game of football: in preparation for a game, NFL teams draw up a custom game plan unique to each game, taking into account various factors such as the opposing team, team members' health, availability of key players, etc. In these game plans, teams script predetermined plays into the opening possessions of games. Most scripts contain approximately 15 plays designed to establish a rhythm, take advantage of a tendency they spot in opponent's defense, engage specific players early on, or use formations to identify defensive coverages by the opposing team.

So, you can see how this analogy extends to an Agile M&A game plan. The Agile game plan consists of a collection of core plays (i.e., processes) that serve as the operational reference guide for the M&A initiative. The game plan also contains a series of optional situational plays (analogous to "audibles") to be executed if specific situations arise during the M&A project. For example, an acquihire will not require the full deck of resources typically used to approach a more involved M&A project; in other cases, an international transaction may emphasize collaboration between remote team members and demand specific resources or tools to facilitate that teamwork.

This modular approach allows the project team to adapt to changing scenarios in order to optimize team performance and minimize delays. If an integration effort is expected to be more complex than usual for any reason, the team can develop a plan to accommodate more situational plays. Most projects, regardless of size and scope, should develop a risk response plan. M&A integration teams benefit from "audibles," which allow the project team to make "on-the-field" adjustments within the guidelines set by the game plan. The deal lead and deal project manager will be equipped with the tools to decide whether certain situations warrant ad-hoc adjustments. The game plan gives autonomy to the team, enabling quick decisions without reliance on rigid escalation protocols, which often lead to costly delays. In short:

1. Agile's modular play-based game plan allows for a quick response to changing conditions; situational plays emphasize preparedness and reduce risk.
2. The game plan facilitates management of parallel workstreams and multiple teams through all stages of integration.
3. Flexibility of the Agile framework improves collaboration and communication between teams, reducing delays and keeping costs down.

THE AGILE M&A PROCESS MODEL

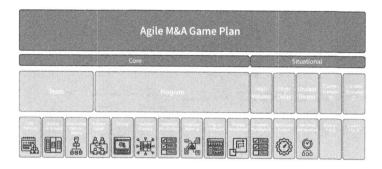

Additional resources for building a Game Plan available at agilema.com

To implement a tailored approach to M&A and maximize the benefits of Agile, the following key steps serve as a guideline for constructing a custom Game Plan:

1. Assess core processes and situational needs for the project.
2. Evaluate team-level processes and procedures; identify key plays that are expected to optimize team performance.
3. Evaluate program-level processes and procedures; identify key plans that enhance program visibility and risk identification.
4. Brainstorm potential scenarios that may increase the risk of project success; develop specific risk response plans, i.e., custom plays.

Next, we will look at some of the core Agile plays that can be tested and configured for your game plan.

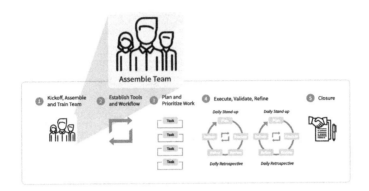

Play #1: Kickoff Meeting

The first play in the M&A process is a site of difficulty for many organizations: conducting an effective kickoff of the formal diligence phase of the project. The preliminary stages of the deal culminate in the kickoff, which marks the formalized intent to buy or sell a company, and the deal officially leaves the drawing board. The kickoff is a critical moment for establishing the tone and momentum of the deal process in a larger sense.

A well-planned and well-executed kickoff elevates the morale of the deal team and promotes confidence both internally and externally. A botched kickoff can have the opposite effect and cast a shadow over the entire M&A project. On a more pragmatic level, teams leave good kickoff meetings informed, aligned, and with clarity regarding their roles, duties, and overarching end goals. The kickoff accordingly plays a crucial role in enabling a team to operate in an Agile manner.

The deal lead drives the kickoff meeting. Representatives from the corp dev team and the deal PM play supporting roles as needed. At the broadest level, the meeting is meant to ensure that everyone involved in the M&A initiative shares a common understanding of the project and of their roles. The meeting should cover a number of topics in detail, including the following:

1. Overview of the target asset (who are they? What business are they in? Where are they located?) and the acquisition strategy (why this company?)
2. Conditions for success (what specific goals and targets do we need to realize in order for this initiative to be successful?)
3. Any challenges, risks, or concerns which have already been identified
4. Other relevant information uncovered by corp dev during preliminary due diligence
5. Milestones, roles, and duties for due diligence (that is, who needs to do what, and by when)
6. Milestones, roles, and duties for integration planning
7. Who can communicate with the target asset, and under what circumstances
8. How the deal team will work together (what tools will we use? How will we communicate? What plays will we run?)

The kickoff meeting provides the deal team with a good opportunity to determine the cadence of meetings and to establish expectations for any work to be completed before the next meeting. The kickoff also grants the PM a platform to outline their expectations regarding workflow and processing and to supply details on tools and training.

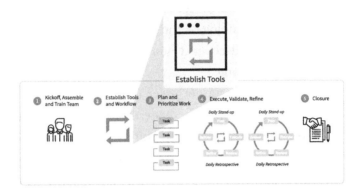

ESTABLISHING TECH TOOLS

When it comes to selecting tech tools, choosing web-based collaborative software platforms can help teams realize the Agile goals of cross-functional visibility, collaborative workflow, and comprehensive information access. During due diligence, the choice of the data room will likely be out of the deal team's hands — but the team can nevertheless establish internal project management and communication tools to use throughout the process.

Using the same suite of tools in task tracking and communication throughout the entire M&A lifecycle alleviates many of the old headaches and obstacles associated with Excel and email, and helps to transmit the information uncovered during due diligence over to the integration effort. Tool Setup Checklist:

- Create accounts
- Configure access rights for each account
- Create custom workflow for project and customized statuses for the process flow
- Provide walkthrough/training for workflow

The kickoff meeting is, moreover, a good opportunity

for the deal PM to determine which additional plays to field during the diligence process. The Agile M&A Process recommends that any M&A project, no matter the circumstances, should involve plays such as frequent standup meetings, a prioritized backlog of tasks, and periodic team retrospectives. These plays will be detailed below.

Although the kickoff meeting represents a relatively small segment of the Agile M&A Process, it is essential in establishing team alignment. The kickoff play provides the framework enabling the deal team to complete the M&A process in an Agile manner.

Tips and Pointers:
The kickoff meeting can be scaled down and run by small groups addressing subprocesses within a larger project. The small-scale kickoff is especially useful during post-merger integration, when numerous small teams will be working on independent projects in parallel. Augmenting a team-wide integration kickoff meeting with smaller functional kickoffs allows alignment to grow from both the bottom up and the top down simultaneously.

Key Takeaways:
- Value Proposition: holding an effective kickoff meeting brings teams into alignment, which leads to a more effective project execution
- How to put it in play:
    » Communicate the vision
    » Define the key objectives

» Provide the team with a mechanism for improving the process with each iteration
- Anti-patterns to avoid:
   » Information silos and/or bottlenecks
   » Inefficient information management
   » Only involving "experts" in decision-making

Play #2: Standup Meeting

During transactions, new information, responsibilities, and dependencies arise constantly. Without proper team communication and collaboration, these emergent conditions can easily block important deal progress and lead to irreversible miscalculations. Establishing an effective cadence of meetings between team members to foster sufficient communication is therefore vital to deal success.

In traditional project teams, it is common practice for the entire team to meet once a week to discuss progress, as well as to address any developing challenges or issues. The project manager usually leads the meeting and collects status information from each individual. Structuring meetings in this way is laborious, and an inefficient use of time; often the topics of discussion are not relevant to many members of the team, who nevertheless must take time out of their workday to attend.

When meetings are only conducted once a week, updates tend to be long, and important issues easily become diluted. Meetings are often not organized in a way that fosters cross-functional collaboration, as they are not thoughtfully structured and attended by those team members who can collaborate on dependencies. If additional meetings are called during the week, it is usually to address a problem. Waiting to address an issue not only creates further complications, but also prolongs project timelines and slows important progress.

By contrast, Agile teams commonly to hold a short meeting at the beginning of each workday, usually known as a "daily standup." The standup meeting helps to maintain a high degree of alignment established by the kickoff meeting. During a standup, every team member gives a brief description of what they are currently working on, focusing on challenges and areas with dependencies.

This meeting enhances communication and cross-functional visibility and helps to keep everyone working a deal aligned with each other while encouraging collaboration to address challenges. Holding a brief meeting once a day affords the team the opportunity to identify and address issues early, preventing minor concerns from growing into major problems.

Expert Opinions:

"I've worked very fast-moving deals and I had a standup with the CEO every morning to talk about the top things that I know that my team's going to ask for today. Immediately after meetings with the CEO, I had one with my cross-functional teams to kind of bookend them. We kind of got rid of checklists because we just had conversations, and I usually followed up with an email about the three or five things we need to focus on today. That was a really

> fast-moving deal here at Google and that was how we got it done."
>
> —James Harris, Principal of Corporate Development Integration at Google

Ultimately, every business, team, and deal is unique. In many instances, it may be unnecessary, counterproductive, or simply logistically impossible to conduct standups on a daily basis. If you find this to be the case, try moving the meetings to every other day, or holding them bi-weekly. The objective is to set a cadence that meets your team's immediate operational needs.

The regular cadence of the standup was developed as a direct response to conventional meetings, which are often only held "as needed." Conventional meetings are often called only after a problem arises and needs to be addressed, and, as a result, these meetings tend to be lengthy and negative in tone.

Teams that assemble daily at standup meetings, however, are better equipped to anticipate and work collaboratively to solve problems that may arise, which ensures a smooth workflow and more positive interactions. The regular cadence of meetings also allows individual team members to maintain an up-to-date picture of their colleagues' workflows, which in turn makes it possible for the team to function in a truly Agile manner.

Whether or not standups are held daily, they should be routine and conducted in closely spaced intervals as is consistent with the Agile approach.

THE AGILE M&A PROCESS MODEL

When organizing a standup, consider following this structure:
1. Establish a time and place for the project team to meet, preferably in the morning. Encourage employees to remain standing during the meeting to improve focus, engagement, and succinctness.
2. Have each attendee share the current status of their work, focusing on items that require help from others. Typically, team members are asked to briefly answer three questions:
    - What did I complete since our last meeting?
    - What will I be working on until our next meeting?
    - What challenges am I facing?

Ideally, each team member reflects on what they need to discuss before the meeting begins. This helps to keep each individual contribution succinct and minimizes the likelihood that speakers will accidentally omit important information. By preparing points to be discussed, team members will also be more focused on what their colleagues have to say, without the distraction of preparing their own talking points on the spot. When a team member describes a challenge they face, they should be prepared to identify other team members that may be able to provide assistance. The relevant individuals should then coordinate after the standup to determine an appropriate course of action.

Expert Opinions:
"As a team, you should talk to each other once a day. Talk to each other when things are going well and when things are not going well. The anti-pattern is

> only talking to each other when things are failing, so it is always tense and stressful. Somebody is always blaming somebody for not having done something or not having done something properly. That creates bad relationships. Imagine that you only talked to your significant other when something was going wrong — this is all negative feedback all the time. That is not the basis of a successful relationship. The same is true for work teams. If you only talk to each other when things are going wrong, it is all negative feedback all the time and it is not the basis of a good relationship or good results."
>
> —*M&A Science Interview with Richard Kasperowski, Author, Consultant, and Harvard University instructor*

The duration of the standup can vary considerably based upon the number of members in the group and the nature of their work. Ten to fifteen minutes is sufficient in most cases. Some meetings can take longer, but the team should avoid meetings running on for more than half an hour. Keeping the standup short and succinct helps team members align and coordinate, without cutting significantly into their workday. Even when conducted daily, standups are meant to ultimately save time by limiting the need for those lengthy traditional meetings and by solving issues before they arise.

Tips and Strategies: The key to an effective daily standup is to keep it as short, informative, and free-flowing as possible.

Long and disorganized meetings are notorious attention-killers. For successful standups, try the following techniques:
1. **Set a routine.** If meetings are called only "as needed," the team falls into a pattern of waiting for a problem to arise before a meeting can occur. The purpose of the standup is to meet regularly to best adapt to the evolving needs of your team, and to anticipate issues before they become problematic.
2. **Remain standing.** It is called the "standup" for a reason! When everyone is seated, meetings are likely to drag on and team members will lose focus.
3. **Keep your share relevant to the team as a whole.** One-on-one talks can happen anytime throughout the workday. Team members selected during the standup to provide assistance on certain tasks can coordinate with each other once the meeting concludes.
4. **Keep your PM tool visible.** Maintaining visibility ensures that everyone is aware of the current state of the project and remains engaged with the PM tool.

In some working environments, it may not be possible for team members to physically meet at regular intervals. Whether spread throughout a building, different cities, or across the globe, teams will need to employ tech tools to hold their standups. A quick morning conference call or video chat works well in this situation. Some teams even opt for a dedicated channel within a chat tool, such as Slack.

For a temporary, project-oriented group like a deal team, the standup is critical to fostering an Agile atmosphere. To understand why this is the case, consider the unique challenges presented by the M&A process. Due diligence and integration are highly informationally complex. For the sake of convenience, teams tend to organize checklists by functional areas. In reality, however, any company almost always has a complex and intricate network of dependencies running between functional groups.

When teams work in silos, these dependencies can be overlooked. This holds true not only in the context of M&A but for all cross-functional corporate projects — and managers often strive to "break down the walls" between silos to encourage cross-functional visibility.

It is important to be attuned to dependencies from an early stage. Begin the project by kicking off an analysis regarding the standard dependencies that occur in every acquisition, as well as the particular dependencies unique to this acquisition. It is rare that further dependencies will be identified later following a thorough analysis at the outset. Laying out dependencies in this way ensures that the team will resolve them.

While it's easy to talk about "breaking down silos," meaningful cross-functional visibility is very difficult to achieve. A team must meet two preliminary conditions to realize true cross-functional visibility:

- Every team member must have a general understanding of the roles played in the project by the other members of their team.
- Every team member must be aware of the current progress of different functions.

The standup provides a structure for realizing these criteria simply and effectively. The constant flow of up-to-date information from each area helps individual team members to develop a detailed picture of the project as it evolves. In turn, this helps each individual to understand the role of their work in relation to their team members and to contextualize their contribution within the project as a whole. A team empowered by this type of mutual insight and shared vision is extremely effective and is capable of spotting challenges and dependencies invisible to more traditional teams.

Moreover, the standup is extremely simple to apply. Detailed knowledge of Agile principles is not necessary to run an effective standup. The concept can be explained to any employee in a few minutes, and conducting the standup itself requires a very small investment.

Key Takeaways:
- Value Proposition: holding an effective standup meeting reveals issues and risks early, and promotes teamwork
- How to put it in play:
  » Communicate the objectives
  » Share successes and obstacles
  » Coach the team to solve problems quickly and to ask for help where needed
- Anti-patterns to avoid:
  » Excessive analysis or problem-solving during standup
  » Delaying escalation of impediments
  » Continuing to work a problem for several days instead of asking for assistance

AGILE M&A

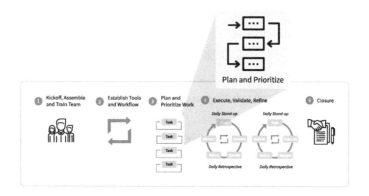

Play #3: Prioritized Backlog

Managing the incredibly complex system of emerging responsibilities while making sure all team members are focused on the highest priority tasks as deal goals fluctuate, is one of the greatest daily challenges M&A practitioners face. Concentrating important collaborative efforts on constantly changing priorities is luckily an undertaking well addressed by Agile through a backlog technique.

Maintenance of a quality backlog is critical to team-wide collaboration. The prioritized backlog is all about how the team approaches the work itself, whereas plays like the kickoff meeting and the daily standup primarily serve to create and maintain the team dynamic fundamental to the Agile Process Model. Using a unified backlog presents an improvement over Excel, in terms of enhanced visibility and facilitating collaboration more effectively in real time. Sending Excel spreadsheets back and forth between team members is time-consuming and opens up vulnerability to errors, but utilizing a backlog management tool expedites and streamlines the information exchange process.

The prioritized backlog emerged from the "Kanban" board, which itself originated from a Japanese manufacturing process.

Dictionary: *Kanban.* Toyota developed Kanban — meaning "signpost" in Japanese — to address workflow issues. In Kanban, a project team places a whiteboard in a highly visible area where team members congregate. The whiteboard is then divided into four areas: a "backlog" or "to do" area, a "priority" or "next up" area, an "in progress" area, and a "completed" area. A process to be completed is broken up into many smaller items or subprocesses. These subprocesses are written out on slips of paper and placed in the "to do" area of the board. The team then works collaboratively to move cards forward through the subsequent areas of the board. The Kanban board gives members an intuitive visual indicator of the current state of the project, and helps to identify which areas need attention.

Many Agile methodologies organize their workflow according to the principles of Kanban. The organizational specifics vary, and most teams now rely on PM software in place of a physical board, but the goal remains the same: to provide employees with a collaborative and immediate visually intuitive overview of the progress of the project.

Expert Opinions:

"Kanban (backlog) is really useful when you're dealing with a client situation where there's a lot going on during integration. So you're pulling people who are

> also doing new product development, there's a new strategy over there, there's a new market entry over there. So you need to be very flexible and not set up unachievable goals because you need to understand that everyone you're working with is being pulled left, right, and center. So Kanban can be particularly useful in that kind of environment."
>
> — *David Boyd, Founding Partner of Agile Gorilla*

To create a backlog, a project team collaborates to break the larger project up into small, actionable work items. Collectively, these individual tasks form the project backlog. The team should organize the backlog in order of importance. In some cases, cross-functional tasks, and tasks with many dependencies take precedence over low-level or monofunctional tasks.

In other instances, certain monofunctional tasks are serial and need to be accomplished first, for reasons pertaining to timing. Think about a fully integrated project timeline: some items must be addressed first in order for others to be successfully completed. Typically, all team members work on different tasks in parallel.

THE AGILE M&A PROCESS MODEL

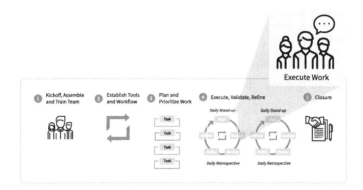

The preliminary breakdown and prioritization of a project follow the kickoff. The deal lead or project manager assigns initial tasks to different team members during the kickoff meeting. As the project evolves, team members report on their progress with various work items during standups. Teams may opt to maintain a physical copy of the priority backlog in their meeting area to track progress, but the primary backlog should be organized on a collaborative PM platform.

As the project progresses, the project team should periodically reprioritize the backlog to reflect emerging project conditions and challenges, keeping the highest priority items near the top of the list whenever possible. Continual reassessment of the sequence will help the team remain focused on the acquisition strategy, eliminate unnecessary or repetitive work, and avoid losing sight of the big picture.

> **Expert Opinions:**
> "I have seen people get checklist fever, which basically means they are not stepping back and thinking about [the big picture]. Pilots have rigorous pre-flight checklists, but the pilot also walks around the aircraft and does a general assessment outside of the checklist to make sure that they are ready to fly. I think the same thing should happen with normal processes. A good quote comes to mind, 'if everybody is thinking the same way, then someone is not thinking,' and I think that is a good way to look at a checklist. If everybody is thinking about the checklist, then someone is not thinking about what is not on the checklist."
>
> —*James Harris, Principal of Corporate Development Integration at Google*

THE PRIORITIZED BACKLOG FOR DILIGENCE

Managing details and ensuring that everyone is working on the highest priority tasks throughout the deal process is one of the largest challenges in M&A.

Priorities are in flux throughout the deal as new situations arise and conditions shift. In order to keep track during the process, tasks are tagged as a high priority on diligence or integration trackers, then shared with the team and counterparties so that everyone involved knows what to focus on. As the number of items tagged as high priority grows, however, half the list could be considered a "top priority." The list becomes meaningless, and the team's valuable time and efforts become disorganized.

Maintaining lists of tasks in descending order of priority, visible to your team and appropriate stakeholders, develops a focus on top tasks that keeps the deal moving forward through evolving variables and distractions. In any project, regardless of scale, keeping a list of highest priorities and tracking progress is critical to a successful outcome. Although this seems intuitive and painfully obvious, the traditional approach to M&A deals often excludes a centralized list that updates in real-time for all practitioners to view and track. A project management platform makes it easy to change the order of priorities as deals evolve and new information emerges.

This type of prioritized list is often referred to as a backlog. With a centralized backlog organized in this way, teams can react quickly to new requests or changing priorities; the backlog allows for clarity and agility in collaboration on big-picture goals.

As the deal team processes documents, they inevitably discover accounting errors and information gaps, which require additional requests issued to the target company. The Agile M&A process acknowledges that the parameters of complex projects like due diligence invariably fluctuate. Prioritization of new requests/work items on a regular basis ensures that the team addresses the highest priority items in a timely manner. While the specific process for handling prioritization varies depending on the size and complexity of each deal, the following are a few solutions to consider.

OPTION 1 - DAILY PRIORITIZATION

For large deals managing a high volume of requests, daily

prioritization may be necessary to ensure the data within the backlog reflects the current priorities.

OPTION 2 - WEEKLY PRIORITIZATION

For deals with a more moderate volume of diligence requests, teams may find prioritizing the backlog on a weekly basis more effective. A weekly approach provides a simple structure to ensure that requests are reviewed and sequenced accordingly, but at the same time allows for expedited processes to occur if an urgent request enters the workflow.

OPTION 3 - ON-DEMAND PRIORITIZATION

Special requests or urgent, unexpected needs discovered during an M&A project must be managed in an organized fashion. The newly-revealed needs should be prioritized against known work items, in order to evaluate priority.

Key Takeaways:
- Value Proposition: building and maintaining a prioritized backlog ensures that the team is focused on the most important work and on identifying critical issues as early as possible
- How to put it in play:
  » Review the backlog regularly
  » Add/update the backlog to reflect latest priorities
  » Pull work from the top of the backlog, as a general rule
- Anti-patterns to avoid:
  » Adding work without sufficient understanding of the larger goals

» Prioritize work only when an emergency situation is identified

Play #4: Team Retrospective

Truly developing and maintaining a culture of continuous improvement and refinement is difficult to achieve, yet vital for M&A functions to deliver reliable maximum value. Implementing retrospectives, a fundamental Agile practice, can enable practitioners to extract important lessons from M&A deals and proactively enforce them to improve future outcomes.

Retrospectives are meetings that take place during deal milestones or after the deal closes, to review what is working well and what is not, as well as to consider how to improve on the process. The goal of retrospectives is to gauge the effectiveness of deal processes and tools and to determine a plan for future improvement. These open discussions help to identify ways to improve processes and strengthen team alignment. Morale increases overall when team members feel that their voices are heard, and team members will likely have great follow-through on ideas they generate themselves.

To put the retrospective into play, set time to meet with your team, and send the questions you will ask ahead of time so that team members can reflect and prepare their responses should include: "What worked really well for this deal?" "What lessons have we learned that we can apply to the next deal?" and "What did not work this time that we should avoid doing on this next deal?"

> **Expert Opinions:**
> "Retrospectives are probably the most valuable thing. Have you ever worked on a project that lasted many months, maybe even more than a year, and at the end of it did a thing called a postmortem? Usually either you give each other high-fives and move on, or you complain about all the things that did not go well and you move on. Nothing changes, you just start the next project. You do all the same things that you did last time, whether they were good or bad. It is ineffective. 'Postmortem' means 'after death.' They are held after the project is already dead, so they have no impact on [the current] project and they really have no impact on the next project, because it will involve a different configuration of people, a different team, and they are not getting feedback fast enough to actually learn effectively and make changes.
> One of the typical Agile practices is to do feedback sessions with the team, called 'retrospectives.' Do a retrospective every one or two weeks, look at what is happening, look at ways to help the team be more effective, look for ways to unlock the team's latent value and the organization's latent value."
> — *M&A Science Interview with Richard Kasperowski, Author, Consultant and Harvard University instructor*

Conduct the meeting and emphasize the importance of openness. Then, summarize the meeting's key conclusions and commitments for improvement. Holding retrospectives will not only improve your next deal but will also build a strong culture of trust and collaboration.

The retrospective presents the opportunity for the team to reflect back on their process periodically and to extract useful lessons. The conclusions drawn from the retrospective meeting are integrated into the process before the next meeting — proven processes are replicated, and problems re-examined and evaluated. By closely examining poor processes, participants brainstorm new approaches to replace these ineffective procedures. Through this thoughtful periodic evaluation, the group as a whole engages in a process of continuous evaluation and improvement.

Most traditional projects follow a process called the "project post-mortem," also known as "lessons learned." If the project was successful, the project post-mortems takes the form of a big celebration — but, if not, it becomes a "witch hunt." In either case, future improvements to the process are seldom the central focus.

> **Expert Opinions:**
> "Do a retrospective every one or two weeks to look at what's happening and look at ways to help the team be more effective. Look for ways to unlock the team's latent value and the organization's latent value and do that every week or every two weeks. If you have one idea every week for how to make the team or company better, by the end of the year you've had 52 ideas. It's not just that you had 52 ideas and you fixed 52 things, the first idea from the first week is sort of compounding interest and the interest on having

> made that improvement will compound throughout the rest of the year. You'll get greater and greater benefits throughout the year. By the end of the year, you've had 52 ideas to make things better and you've had all the compounding interest from the 52 weeks. The team and the organization are going to be so much better of doing that versus doing a postmortem at the end of the 12th month."
> — *M&A Science Interview with Richard Kasperowski, Author, Consultant and Harvard University instructor*

The Agile retrospective is different and is designed to focus squarely on refining and improving the deal process, the meeting takes place periodically over the course of the M&A project.

During the retrospective, the team should engage in the following:

1. Highlight issues that affect workflow and team dynamic
2. Analyze the effectiveness of any plays fielded, and brainstorm potential adjustments
3. Discuss how successful the team has been in aligning low-level work with the True North strategic goals of the initiative
4. Review any other pertinent items affecting the deal team or the diligence process

The ultimate goal of the team retrospective is to provide a foundation for continuous improvement. In most cases, the core members of a deal team will work with each other over the course of the entire M&A lifecycle, and work together again on future deals. If they can effectively refine and improve their team dynamic and workflow with each project, the team will gradually evolve towards an ideal operating state.

Key Takeaways:
- Value Proposition: holding an effective retrospective encourages the team to seek to accomplish tasks in a more efficient and effective way
- How to put it in play:
  » Examine successes as well as opportunities for improvement
  » Consider key dimensions such as people, processes, and tools
  » Commit to making at least one change for the next logical increment of time (e.g. per sprint/iteration or per month)
- Anti-patterns to avoid:
  » Focusing excessively on negatives or positives
  » Continuing to do things the same way and expecting different results
  » Considering ideas only from the most senior or experienced team member

CLOSE THE DEAL; INCORPORATE FINAL LESSONS

Once the deal team has begun to receive a steady flow of information from the target asset, the team naturally establishes a daily cadence of planning, executing, reviewing, refining, and delivering work items. As the team completes tasks, the total volume of remaining work items continuously decreases.

If a deal makes it through the diligence period without the deal team uncovering any major issues, the acquisition is almost sure to go ahead. Between lawyers, advisors, bankers, and data room providers, the diligence process often costs millions of dollars — if either party walks away, it is inevitably both costly and demoralizing to everyone involved. But regardless of how the deal plays out, the role of the deal team in its conventional form ends with diligence.

Following the close of the deal, Agile team members should take some time to think about the deal process as a whole, asking questions like: "what worked really well for this deal?" and "what lessons have we learned that we can apply to the next deal?" and "what did not work this time that we should avoid in the next deal?"

Once every team member has had sufficient time to reflect, the deal team should close out the diligence project and formally initiate the next phase of the M&A lifecycle: post-merger integration. The same set of Agile practices used in the deal itself can scale to accommodate the more complex needs of the integration process.

POST-MERGER INTEGRATION

Play #5: Parallel Planning for Integration

When approaching a deal and assembling the teams involved, always remember: **the earlier integration staff are brought into a deal, the more likely the deal is to meet its ultimate objectives.** The integration lead's involvement ideally begins at the earliest strategic meetings outlining the initiative itself and extends through the conclusion of the M&A process.

During the pre-close phase of the deal, the role of the integration lead is to (1) **provide a tactical perspective** to the business development and deal teams, and (2) **create a detailed post-merger integration plan** to be executed on day one.

THE POST-MERGER INTEGRATION PLAN

A strong post-merger integration plan contains two basic components: an **integration charter** outlining the high-level goals and parameters of the project, and **step-by-step checklists** detailing the individual tasks required to integrate different workstreams at the tactical level.

The charter outlines the nature of the integration, including its purpose, deliverables, success criteria, and budget. Additionally, the charter includes a list of the resources and personnel required for execution of the integration, establishes a preliminary timeline, and defines any end-state requirements. The charter should be created immediately upon selecting an individual target, and updated and refined as new information emerges. It falls to the integration team and any pertinent outside constituencies to continuously validate the charter and maintain alignment with the project goals.

According to the strategy outlined by the charter, relevant functional experts develop detailed step-by-step checklists, outlining the tactical approach to integration. The scope and amount of low-level work required during integration vary considerably, depending upon different strategic considerations, namely the level of integration to take place: are you partly integrating this company? Fully integrating? Or not integrating at all?

With countless possible integration configurations, the more time integration specialists have to consider the many variables governing their project, the stronger the post-merger integration plan.

Tips and Strategies: The deal team is inherently cross-functional. The overwhelming majority of the tasks the team completes over the course of the project include component elements from multiple workstreams. Encouraging individual team members to deepen their understanding of the needs and duties of their colleagues empowers the team as a whole to carry out its duties more effectively.

"I have encouraged teams as part of a regular transaction to pick a domain and spend a little bit more time with that domain to understand their processes and how they work. I have asked multiple times for integration teams and integration managers to spend a period of time just leaning in. Like, 'on this deal I want you to spend a little bit more time with the HR team to understand how we set compensation, how we set levels, how we set promotion cycles,' so that they understand that world a little better and are more conscious of its needs. That way, if we are going to do something that is impactful we can raise it with them earlier and give that time team a little bit more lead time. You have to be an M&A ambassador to those teams and figure out how to work a thoughtful solution that still supports the deal but does not drive over some of the other teams."

—*James Harris, Principal of Corporate Development Integration at Google*

Preliminary planning for the transaction begins before the signing of the LOI. An acquiring company should clarify its assumptions about how and why the integration needs to occur, and justify the pursuit of the deal at the proposed valuation. When an LOI is signed with the chosen target company, the formal due diligence period begins.

As diligence progresses, the deal team can use the information unveiled to continuously refine and add detail to the post-merger integration plan. The team should also look ahead to potential cultural issues, design customer and market strategies, and generally perform as much preparatory work as possible. When the deal is formally closed, the deal team can approach the integration stage prepared and well-informed.

> **Expert Opinions:**
> "Our role starts during diligence. We are working and forming ideas, understanding the product, the customer market, etc. We use that [information] to determine what we are trying to do with this acquisition—what is the problem we are solving? What is the technology we are building, buying or integrating? We go through an iterative approach throughout the entire company from the front end, where we ask 'how are we going to sell it?', to the back end, where we ask 'how are we going to build it?' We are continually iterating on the integration plan as we find more information."
>
> — *Christina Amiry, Head of M&A Strategic Operations at Atlassian*

The post-merger approach outlined above does not merely bridge the gap between the diligence and post-close integration stages of the M&A lifecycle but eliminates this rift entirely. Realistically, however, maintaining a dedicated integration team is only possible for large serial acquirers, due to cost. Occasional acquirers need to take a different approach.

In many cases, executing integration planning as a parallel workstream during due diligence confers many benefits, such as efficient knowledge-sharing and deeper domain understanding of the deal. Improved outcomes emerge from team members' ability to convey lessons learned during due diligence across to the Integration team, which significantly accelerates the overall integration timeline and leads to significant reductions in cost and time spent.

THE AGILE M&A PROCESS MODEL

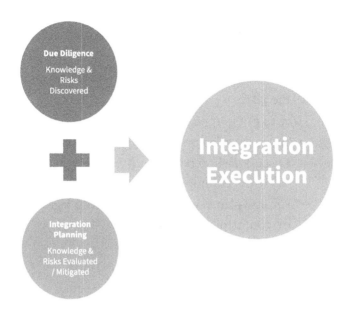

Tips and Strategies: Developing the overall integration plan needs to be an iterative process because, as more information is learned about the entities to be consolidated, new issues and opportunities may present themselves and the integration goals may need to adapt to the specific circumstances. As the goals change, more fact-gathering may be required to assess their feasibility and implications. With each iteration, however, the objectives of the integration and the best way to achieve those objectives should come more sharply into focus, producing a more detailed and refined plan.
—*Baker Mckenzie Post-Acquisition Integration Handbook*

Key Takeaways:
- Value Proposition: planning the project with multiple teams optimizes communication, and allows all team members to contribute to the development of the plan
- How to put it in play:
  » Invite interdependent teams to complete tasks
  » Discuss task dependencies and key milestones, to ensure common understanding
  » Create a plan in which all teams have a high degree of confidence
- Anti-patterns to avoid:
  » Focusing only on a single teams' tasks
  » Not sharing the plan with other teams
  » Creating a plan with too many variables and/or external dependencies and unknowns

DAY ONE

The next phase of the M&A lifecycle, the formal integration process, begins on "day one." Following the successful execution of pre-integration, integration should be starting off on the best possible footing: with a clearly defined vision of the target asset, and a detailed blueprint for the integration process. No matter the size of the transaction, the post-merger integration process invariably entails more work, more dedicated personnel, and a much greater degree of operational complexity than diligence.

The integration process commonly involves numerous teams working simultaneously to integrate different functions. Keeping all of these teams aligned, within scope, and on schedule presents a serious managerial undertaking — and, in general, integration specialists talk and think about project management far more than do their colleagues in corporate development.

In companies with an established integration management strategy, a department called the Integration Management Office (IMO) usually coordinates large integrations involving multiple functional teams. In other cases, the IMO is a temporary project management office created to oversee the integration process, set up during diligence at LOI, or sometimes even earlier in the process. Serial acquirers, however, often have a permanent IMO running continuously. The IMO owns the integration plan, coordinates the different teams involved, manages cross-functional dependencies, and tracks the progress of the project as a whole.

As the driving force behind the process, the IMO plays a critical role in the Agile M&A Process Model. The IMO owns the integration charter and is responsible for coordinating the tactical teams completing the step-by-step checklists. A well-run IMO helps to keep the project on target, reduce dependency issues, enable ground level teams to creatively solve emerging problems, and generally maximizes the likelihood that integration projects realize their True North objectives.

The deal team establishes and runs the IMO, and, as previously described, the deal team is composed of the integration lead and functional experts representing the different workstreams impacted by the integration initiative. In theory, each of these experts also serves as the team leader of the functional group in charge of completing the checklist covering their workstream. This creates a hierarchical structure ensuring strategic decisions are made by a team with comprehensive, up-to-date knowledge of tactical conditions and challenges on the ground level.

Both the IMO and functional teams can support efficient workflow and alignment by fielding the same plays used by the deal team during diligence. Since the scale of the integration project is so much larger than the diligence project, however, the plays must be scaled up as well.

Play #6: Integration Kickoff

HOLDING A KICKOFF FOR INTEGRATION

Given the greater number of personnel typically involved in integration, holding a project-wide kickoff meeting is not a particularly effective means of encouraging alignment. In general, it makes the most sense for each individual team to hold its own small kickoff.

The deal team holds the first of these kickoff meetings, to discuss strategic alignment, establish workflow and assign initial tasks, and ensure that each team member has the resources they need to assist subteams.

Traditionally, the integration process is conducted by functional—that is, siloed—teams, which are aligned at the higher levels by the IMO. Since the deal team consists of functional experts covering the breadth of the new asset, its members can serve as the leads of the relevant functional teams. The traditional functional-driven workstreams limits information shared between teams, and the overlap in workstreams can result in duplicate requests and efforts with the target company. This can be one of the most frustrat-

THE AGILE M&A PROCESS MODEL

ing aspects of the process for a company being integrated. Completing the integration process using cross-functional, goal-oriented teams is an innovative new strategy employed by some companies in the tech industry. In this approach, the IMO establishes a number of high-level tasks that must be completed in order to close out the integration effort. The IMO then assembles small, cross-functional teams containing all the personnel required to complete that task. The IMO coordinates these teams like they would traditional functional teams.

Whichever strategy your team follows, once the IMO is set up and the deal team aligned, the members of the team can assemble their subteams and consequently lead project kickoffs. Each subteam lead should begin by outlining to their team the nature of the new asset, the ultimate goals of the M&A initiative, and the strategy the IMO has developed to realize those goals. The subteam leaders should then define the role of their team in relation to the project, describe the initial tasks to be addressed by the subteam, and present a preliminary checklist.

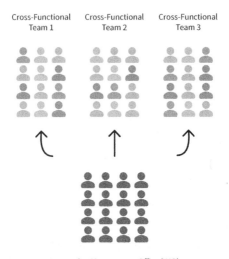

Integration Management Office (IMO)
Serves All Cross-Functional Teams

Rarely does every subteam begin its process on day one. High-level cross-functional dependencies mean that oftentimes certain teams need to complete their initial tasks before other teams are able to begin their work. The deal team is responsible for effectively timing the entry of different teams into the integration project. The overall integration project involves different teams at different stages, and even the composition of individual teams often changes over time as the teams complete tasks. Agile facilitates flexibility and fluidity in team configuration in order to maximize productivity and the efficient use of team resources.

Assuming that the deal team was assembled early on during diligence, the team already has a well-established workflow. The subteams do not have this advantage. The subteams' process method can either be defined by the IMO and enforced by the lead or determined by the team itself. Operating according to the same process and tools

THE AGILE M&A PROCESS MODEL

allows teams to maximize Agile values like cross-functional visibility and collaboration. Compelling functional teams to deviate from their established workflow too radically, however, is likely to cause resentment and resistance, ultimately undermining any desired workflow improvements. One of the great advantages of employing goal-oriented teams is that they are both temporary and cross-functional — however, this does mean that the teams will need to establish a new process in order to operate. The most sensible process for such teams to adopt is that used by the deal team.

Key Takeaways:
- Value Proposition: holding a big kickoff meeting will maximize transparency and engagement for the entire project team
- How to put it in play:
  » Include all project contributors and stakeholders/sponsors
  » Discuss process guidelines and expectations
  » Share key objectives and milestones
- Anti-patterns to avoid:
  » Focusing excessively on specific tasks
  » Solving problems that are not impactful to the overall project
  » Ignoring known risks or issues

Play #7: Multi-team Standup

HOLDING A STANDUP FOR INTEGRATION

A single team often completes due diligence, and this team can hold a straightforward standup. A multi-team project like integration or complex due diligence may require multi-team standups.

We will take integration as an example. All teams actively working the integration project should hold standup meetings to maintain the internal and cross-functional alignment achieved during the integration kickoff.

Since the deal team and their subteams overlap in membership, a schedule of meetings should be created in order to organize and coordinate standup participation.

During the deal team (IMO) standup, each lead briefly outlines what their subteams have been working on, and mentions any upcoming dependencies which will require action from other team members. After this meeting, the leads share any pertinent intel at their subteam standup. If additional cross-functional questions or needs arise during the subteam standup, the lead can address this after the standup concludes.

Play #8: Multi-team Backlog Prioritization

BACKLOG PRIORITIZATION FOR INTEGRATION

Each team begins the integration project with a detailed list of required tasks and deliverables. For the IMO, their task is to be responsible for the integration charter; for the different functional teams, their responsibility is to execute tasks as outlined in the step-by-step checklists. Each team employs these documents to develop their own priority backlog.

The integration charter is already a well-defined document by day one. No charter can ever fully anticipate the complexities and nuances of integration from the start, however. As the integration progresses, the charter is continuously refined as necessary to accommodate emerging conditions on the ground level, and to prevent scope creep. Contingent on the severity of issues discovered, the team may need to adjust the backlog and even recalibrate project timelines.

Recalibration of key elements of the project can have serious consequences, and addressing this issue is beyond the scope of a standup meeting. In such instances, the team should schedule a reprioritization meeting to determine how to keep the project in scope, on budget, and on time.

> **Expert Opinions:**
> "When we close a deal, we set key goals or objectives and then hold 30 day, 60 day, and 90 day check-ins. The intent is to tune those goals. If we are resetting them, then there is a big question regarding why. There may be good reasons, but [altering goals] is always risky, because it means we missed something. To me, that is a big learning opportunity for us to step back and say 'okay, what did we miss? How did we not understand that this was going to take nine months when we thought it was going to take four weeks?' It is [a way to approach] getting better at diligence and integration planning."
> —*James Harris, Principal of Corporate Development Integration at Google*

At the tactical level, the kickoff meeting is the first time most personnel see the functional checklist covering their workstream. A large portion of the kickoff should be devoted to brainstorming alterations, improvements, and potential problems. In all other respects, the backlog can be handled by the functional team in the same manner as it is handled by the IMO: with routine maintenance and updates conducted during the daily standup, and special issues addressed by holding a reprioritization meeting.

Tips and Strategies: Most tasks in the IMO's priority backlog will include components from various workstreams. In order to achieve an ideal workflow project-wide, each component of a cross-functional task must be completed at precisely the right moment. If one team works more quickly than anticipated and reaches a dependent task ahead of schedule, either they must wait for the other teams to catch up, or the other teams must jump ahead in their own backlogs. Conversely, if a team falls behind and fails to complete their task on time, they may hinder many teams at once and jeopardize the project timeline as a whole. To prevent problems like these, the IMO must work tirelessly to keep the backlogs of their functional teams in sync.

Synchronized backlog maintenance presents a significant organizational challenge. The integration team at Atlassian approaches it like the tech innovators that they are: with a powerful collaborative project management software called JIRA. First, they organize the high-level tasks of an integration into a "centralized program backlog." This forms the vertical axis of the project, defining the steps the project will move through over its lifespan. The horizontal axis is comprised of the different workstreams involved. The cross-functional team leading integration maps out the work items required to complete each task on the centralized program backlog across their constituent workstreams. This allows the team to determine the best work order for each functional team from a cross-functional strategic perspective. It also creates a rich, living matrix of information. As functional teams proceed through their backlogs, the IMO can visually track the real-time progress of each workstream.

"We use our own systems and tools [Confluence and Jira] to manage dependencies, define work, and track its progress. Then, on a daily basis, we use communication tools like Slack to do the back and forth design of dependencies and negotiate when things are going to happen so that our timelines line up [and we conduct efficient] resource planning."
—*Christina Amiry, Head of M&A Strategic Operations at Atlassian*

See Plays → Program Dashboard

A printable summary of Agile M&A plays is available at agilema.com

ENDING THE INTEGRATION PROCESS

As the different teams involved in the integration effort work their way through their backlogs, uncertainty decreases. Keeping the charter and functional checklists aligned with the goals of the initiative becomes simpler, as does managing dependencies, and coordinating the project becomes less complex overall. Successfully closing the project within the charter parameters looks increasingly probable.

The integration process does not conclude all at once. Integration ends in the same manner in which it began, with teams gradually closing out their backlogs and exiting the project in a staggered fashion. Only the deal team remains by the very end of the deal. When the deal team finds that all of the end state requirements of the project have been met, the deal lead requests approval from the sponsor of the M&A initiative — generally the CEO or board — to formally close the project. Upon receiving this approval, the deal lead holds its own **project retrospective** to analyze the process and lay the foundation for future improvements.

FORMAL BINDER CLOSE

If the integration project successfully realizes its True North goals, the ending stages of the M&A lifecycle can be a relatively relaxed affair, focusing on potential process and alignment improvements.

In the event that the integration project failed to meet its objectives, this closing period becomes much more hectic and critical. The integration team must take this as a chance to reflect on what went wrong and to come up with potential solutions for future projects. In the unlikely event that the project failed due to incompetence or mismanagement on the side of the integration team, this reflection is largely an internal process. Most integrations fail, however, for reasons beyond the integration team's control.

If the gap between corp dev and integration was not effectively bridged, the integration team may have been handed a fundamentally unworkable asset, or have been expected to meet unrealistic True North goals. Even in cases in which the entire initiative was completed according to best practices — with a dedicated deal team involved from the beginning, a perfectly executed due diligence, and a realistic set of expectations — unforeseen variables could cause the asset to fail to realize its expected potential, or even precipitate a catastrophic failure resulting in the early termination of the integration effort.

Regarding failure, there are three important facts to keep in mind about M&A:

1. Most M&A initiatives fail during integration.
2. This failure typically has nothing to do with the integration team.
3. The integration team is usually blamed for failure anyway.

To make matters worse, when an integration effort succeeds, the integration team's accomplishments usually go unnoticed or unappreciated. By the time the deal is closed, corp dev and the sellers of the acquired business have already celebrated the success of the M&A initiative. If the deal fails post-close, the integration team makes for an easy target. For the integration team, it is a lose-lose situation, and many integration specialists harbor a degree of resentment towards corp dev teams and executives.

An Agile M&A approach neutralizes this disjoint between integration and corp dev from the beginning of the project, by making the case for a true partnership between the two teams — or, ideally, for integration and corp dev to act as a unified team. When both own the process and are tied to long-term outcomes, there is little reason to place blame.

A retrospective to mark the formal close of the M&A project allows for issues that arose during the deal to be considered in a productive way. By presenting a meaningful analysis of precisely what went wrong with the deal, the deal team can clear their name and start a conversation about aligning the two phases of the M&A lifecycle. The post-close retrospective captures lessons learned and generates ideas for improving the process in future iterations.

Once the formal closing process is complete, the deal team officially disbands, and the M&A lifecycle is complete.

Tips and Strategies: There is a well-established inverse relationship between the amount of time an integration takes and the likelihood that it will succeed. Accordingly, it is critical to ensure that integration happens according to a clearly defined schedule. The initial momentum following an acquisition can help to propel a team rapidly through a well-mapped integration strategy.

Around 100-120 days into the process, however, that momentum dwindles, and issues of fatigue and low team morale set in. It is critical to try to hit key goals within this timeframe; some projects, however, will inevitably take longer. A single block or bottleneck can jeopardize the momentum of your integration — a series of complications can destroy value creation entirely.

THE AGILE M&A PROCESS MODEL

To avoid becoming bogged down, it is imperative that teams make every conceivable effort to eliminate unnecessary or repetitive work, communication lags, or other avoidable slowdowns and blockages. This will help to ensure that the complex process of integrating a new asset into the structure of the acquiring company has every possible chance to succeed.

CHAPTER 5

Implementation Strategy for Agile M&A

While Agile is extremely scalable and adaptable, deploying Agile techniques within an organization accustomed to following traditional processes will require commitment to change and strong leadership. Successful adoption challenges the status quo and demands a delicate balance of innovation and organizational change management.

The term "change management" refers to a constellation of techniques designed to help support individuals, teams, and/or companies through significant organizational transformation or restructuring. The M&A process itself relies heavily on change management techniques to help integrate new acquisitions — a process which almost always entails a radical shift in governance and workflow. Teams adopting an Agile approach to M&A initiative can benefit greatly from applying these same techniques. Strong leadership and vision is required to implement change management successfully.

If we are to make the shift to a more transformational and Agile approach to M&A, there needs to also be a similar shift in mindset and behaviors. The way to achieve this is through strong leadership that aligns processes and people. Agility is necessary not only in terms of leadership, in order to facilitate a shift in behaviors, but also in the methods and the tools that you use. Fluidity requires collaboration and openness, a strong focus on early and continuous delivery of value, and a willingness to adapt and a readiness to commit every day. M&A success always begins and ends with leadership. It's the way people own the organization, and look out for and influence each other, that really matters. Agile leadership means working to keep teams aligned and focused on value creation.

Some of the challenges that teams face when attempting to adopt an Agile approach in adoption challenges clude:

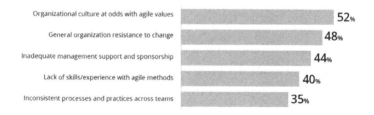

Source: CollabNet/VersionOne

Above is a snapshot from the 13th Annual State of Agile Report, published in 2019. The data shows that it is critical to manage change strategically in order to successfully execute Agile projects. This means that leaders of the organization must be educated in Agile principles so that they can champion and support the change in mindset; without their buy-in and active engagement, the organization will not adopt a new way of doing work and will miss out on an opportunity to gain a competitive edge. Teams will change only if properly motivated, usually by a broader cultural movement.

An organization can successfully apply Agile principles in multiple different ways. Given the uniqueness of each project domain and team, there is no single formula to maximize success. Some companies may adopt specific Agile techniques which advance their unique goals, while others may embrace the process as a whole. Some organizations may already intuitively follow Agile techniques, leaving for a minimal change in process.

Other companies, however, may require larger transformations. In that case, companies may want to approach changes incrementally or adopt them all at once. Despite the current structure of an organization or the implementation approach they choose to take, there are certain strategies that can serve as effective points of reference.

Source: CollabNet/VersionOne

1. Bring in the experts

When a team without previous Agile experience wants to formally adopt an Agile process, the easiest and most painless way is to hire expert advisors to initiate the introduction. Without access to real knowledge and practical experience, any attempt to adopt a radical new process model is sure to devolve into the blind leading the blind.

Luckily, there are many ways to bring that Agile knowledge to the table. An Agile coach can provide training seminars, help teams learn to effectively field plays like the daily standup or prioritizing the backlog, and act as a resource for long-term implementation success.

In some cases, Agile expertise may be more readily accessible than expected. In companies with large IT or software development departments, entire functions may already be operating according to Agile principles. This is how the corp dev and integration teams at Google and Atlassian first started using Agile techniques — by adopting them over time, from the example of other internal company functions.

2. Align teams

The M&A process is primarily about the *movement of information*, and one of the fundamental benefits of Agile is to facilitate that flow. In order for Agile to be applied successfully, however, teams must be aligned. Agile M&A is about breaking down the walls between silos and encouraging the entire deal team to collaborate in real time. It is vital to convey to teams from the outset of the deal that there is an expectation of open communication, organizational transparency, and process alignment. A consistent process allows for teams to communicate needs and challenges instantaneously. This lateral communication between teams eliminates the issue of mediating the flow of information through a third party like a PM, thereby reducing the wait time and stoppages associated with cross-functional dependencies.

Team alignment begins with the kickoff meeting. This is the perfect opportunity to communicate to team members the requirements for team alignment and transparency, and the benefits conferred by such alignment. The constant rhythm of standups and retrospectives reinforces this model. Although functional groups may initially resist complete process alignment due to the increased work inherent in transition and the increased scrutiny under which they will operate, the innumerable workflow advantages will quickly turn the most vocal detractors into advocates.

3. Align tools

Probably the single most important step upper management can take to ensure enhanced *team alignment* is to encourage *tech alignment*. Agile comes out of the software development world, and the entire Agile mindset is built upon the use of new tech tools. E-mail and Excel sheets invariably lead to communication blockages, batch work, and long wait times for information. These outmoded tools should be discarded in favor of group communication platforms like Slack and centralized, collaborative document-sharing platforms and project management tools.

The advantages realized by such a shift are potentially enormous. Research demonstrates that adopting a centralized team chat tool like Slack helps teams to minimize email clutter, and ensures that internal requests are processed quickly. Using a centralized data sharing hub like DealRoom (*dealroom.net*) allows team members to upload requests to a shared platform, where requests can be tagged, viewed, and accessed by anyone — drastically reducing the time and effort required to locate information and coordinate work items.

Tech alignment improves workflow beyond just the front end. The most recent software on the market tracks user behavior information, creating an immensely valuable trove of data that teams can use to identify invisible bottlenecks and blockages, and further refine their processes in future iterations.

4. Lead from the top

A top-to-bottom process overhaul is a huge undertaking and one which will usually encounter some resistance. As an example, let's consider the industry-wide adoption of computerized physician order entry software (CPOE) in hospitals throughout the United States over the last decade. CPOE has been shown to drastically reduce medication errors in hospitals — which has for many years been the most serious threat facing hospitalized persons. CPOE has additionally been demonstrated to improve hospital workflow when properly implemented. Resistance to the new technology among doctors and hospital staff, however, was initially intense, occasionally escalating to the point of "physician rebellion."

The physicians and their staff were upset for three reasons predominantly:
1. They viewed change as fundamentally unnecessary. In their minds, the previous model worked just fine — and, at the end of the day, everyone prefers business as usual.
2. The change was externally imposed by an absent authority.

No one likes being told what to do, and it's not difficult to imagine why resistance developed.
5. The transition involved substantial extra work in the short term.

These three factors combined to create a perfect storm of resentment against the new process. In spite of this unusually extreme resistance, however, CPOE has now been implemented around the nation. This is largely thanks to a combination of strong administrative leadership, the encouragement of leading physicians amongst their peers, and an adoption process that aimed to make the transition as smooth as possible.

TIPS FOR LAUNCHING AN AGILE M&A PROJECT: AGILE M&A QUICKSTART APPROACH

Adopting an Agile approach to deal management is no simple feat. it will require strong sponsorship from the leadership team as well as educated staff to execute the plays in an effective way. The Agile M&A process is designed to be applied in an iterative fashion, which means the team should start with a small set of plays, apply the game plan to gain a practical understanding of how the plays work, then make adjustments with the help from Agile M&A experts who can provide keen insights on taking the team to the next level.

Success may not be achieved immediately, and change will likely feel cumbersome and inefficient at first, but with sustained efforts, most teams will realize significant benefits within a short period of time. The key to developing a sustainable, continuous improvement mindset is to maintain a high level of commitment to the process and to embrace change as the new way of doing business.

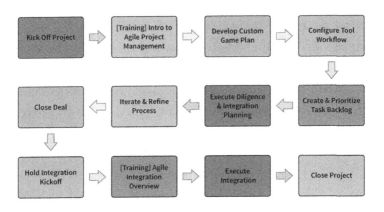

HIGH-LEVEL IMPLEMENTATION ROADMAP

In M&A, successfully managing resistance to process transition should focus on the same goals, and the process is defined largely by *strong executive leadership*. At the kickoff meeting, team leaders should make a case that old models are becoming so outdated that process change is not only desirable but very necessary. Leaders should outline the long-term procedural and workflow benefits they expect the Agile process model to realize, as well as the steps they will take to minimize superfluous work during the transition.

Above all else, leaders should demonstrate their commitment to the Agile model by pursuing training and education in Agile themselves. This will fully position leaders as a part of the team, and furthermore sends a strong message that we are all in this together.

Additional resources for Agile M&A implementation available at **agilema.com**

Conclusion

So, here we are: the end of a book — but only the first steps, for me, of a much longer journey to bring the principles of Agile thinking to the world of M&A. The fact that you picked up this book suggests that you share my view that the current M&A processes are outmoded and in tremendous need of refinement. The fact that you have read this far suggests that you have found my case for agile M&A somewhat convincing.

When I initially began this project, I had compiled a long list of procedural challenges I faced during deals, which I wanted to address. It was only when I started making discovery calls that I realized just how many people shared these pain points at every level of the industry. So, I called around, collected pain points, and began to brainstorm how to use new PM strategies like Agile to overcome them.

My ultimate goal in writing this book is to communicate my enthusiasm about the Agile process, and the possibilities it has for revolutionizing M&A. If I've succeeded in doing this in any way, I've met that goal. If, because of this book, any readers bring up the idea of Agile with a coworker or to the rest of their team at a meeting, I've met my goal. If any readers field an Agile play during a deal or integration, I've met my goal.

I hope that you will join me in my efforts to improve the operational landscape of the M&A world so that together we can bring meaningful change to this exciting industry.

Reference Guide for Customizable Plays

PLAY: Program Kickoff & Alignment

Description: The entire program team (including all project team members) attends a kickoff meeting to encourage alignment.

Objective: Initiate communication with all project team members. Ensure that focus is on project goals, priorities, key milestones, processes & tools, and success criteria.

Technique: During the early stages of an M&A initiative, the Program Manager facilitates the Program Kickoff with the entire project team, including all contributors, consultants, sponsors, and team leads. The meeting establishes clear guidelines on how the team will operate to achieve a successful outcome.

- Define goals/objectives for program/initiative
- Assemble team with members from key functions and/or departments
- Define key program milestones
- Clarify team roles (i.e. sponsors, stakeholders, leaders, etc.)

PLAY: Tool & Workflow Configuration

Description: Program management team establishes the overall standard for process flow.

Objective: Design a custom workflow and toolset that will support the specific needs of the M&A initiative.

Technique: Once the team is aligned on the overall goals and objectives and ready to collaborate, tools such as DealRoom (*dealroom.net*) will be configured and customized to ensure optimal fit to the specific needs of this particular M&A project. Role-based training events are held as needed to augment the initial foundational training to enable adequate level of support for the tools throughout the project. For example, application administrators may require additional knowledge regarding tool management. The project manager may require hands-on coaching to understand how to apply Agile techniques to different team-level events.

- Identify program requirements and constraints
- Consult Agile M&A advisor to customize process flow (e.g. value stream process mapping)
- Establish and configure work management tools (if applicable)
- Establish team communication model

PLAY: Backlog Planning & Prioritization

Description: Program management team reviews project work and prioritizes all action items and deliverables.

Objective: Build the initial program plan and ensure work is sequenced in the proper rank order by priority.

Technique: Once the necessary tools are configured and all required team members have completed initial training sessions, project tasks are collected, aggregated, and organized for all project teams. Representatives from each team collaborate to ensure the Program Backlog is an aggregate of all work items from all teams, and that appropriate priority is assigned to each item. As work is executed and completed, additional work is expected to originate from a number of different sources such as the buyer, consultants, managers, lawyers, etc.

- Identify program deliverables
- Clarify requirements (e.g. contractual obligations)
- Compile consolidated work item list of activities, tasks, and deliverables
- Prioritize work items according to most important attributes (e.g. risk, business value, dependencies with other work items, etc.)

PLAY: Daily Standup

Description: Project team meets regularly to share progress towards goals and escalate issues as needed.

Objective: Ensure clarity of team plan for the day. Identify and eliminate obstacles as soon as possible to maximize progress.

Technique: All team members from each team meet daily to gain agreement on plan for the day. Issues, requests, concerns are discussed and tracked by the Project Lead.

- Identify team goal and deliverables for the day
- Clarify support needs from team members
- Escalate issues as needed

PLAY: Team Retrospective

Description: Project team review processes & tools to identify opportunities for improving efficiency and/or effectiveness.

Objective: Enable teams to inspect current processes and tools, and to identify opportunities for improvement.

Technique: All team members from a single team meet at the end of an iteration (or a predefined project milestone/checkpoint) to review both effective and dysfunctional processes.
- Identify opportunities for improving the processes/tools
- Select one or two improvement ideas to focus on
- Commit to making the improvement by adding corresponding tasks into the backlog

PLAY: Multi-team Planning

Description: All program team members, including project teams from different functional groups/departments, collaborate to establish tactical execution plan.

Objective: Enable all teams to collaborate and identify risks & dependencies across teams, so that a program-level plan can be finalized.

Technique: Team members from all teams meet to review key interaction points for work items requiring support from multiple teams. Teams identify critical dependencies and establish approximate timing of predecessors and successors to minimize risk of delays. Key risks are documented and categorized by response strategy, i.e. avoid, accept, mitigate, or transfer.
- Assemble teams and team leads

- Review consolidated list of work items
- Allocate work items to individual teams based on expertise & skill set
- Identify cross-team dependencies
- Identify risks and define response plan for high probability/high impact risks

PLAY: Multi-team Standup

Description: Team leads (project managers) collaborate on a regular basis to identify cross-team issues and risks.

Objective: Enable all teams to communicate progress and obstacles to encourage efficient resolution of intra-team issues.

Technique: During program execution, one member from each project team meets with other team representatives to discuss successes and challenges. The Program Lead documents and updates the issue log and prioritizes major impediments to Executive Management Team for assistance as needed.

- Establish schedule and location for standup meeting (2 to 3 times per week)
- Identify representatives from each team
- Clarify meeting goal and process flow
- Establish protocol for escalation of critical issues

PLAY: Multi-team Backlog Refinement

Description: During execution, team leads will collaborate to reassess priorities based on overall progress and newly-discovered work items.

Objective: Evaluate new requests and/or unplanned work to redefine overall priority of work items.

Technique: During program execution, typically once every 2 weeks, representatives from each project team hold a meeting to review requests and unplanned work introduced to the initiative. The level of complexity, effort, and uncertainty for each request is discussed in detail. A priority level is assigned for each new request; if the request is urgent, current work in progress may be deprioritized to allow team members to dedicate time to the new request.

- Identify new requests and/or requirements received since the previous planning session
- Clarify priority and urgency of new requests
- Evaluate impact to current project teams; communicate any changes to current planned work

PLAY: Multi-team Retrospective

Description: Team leads collaborate to evaluate and discuss opportunities for improving current processes & tools that affect multi-team execution.

Objective: Review effectiveness of the processes and tools to determine a plan for future improvement.

Technique: At the end of each iteration, representatives from each team hold a meeting to discuss the level of effectiveness of existing processes and toolset. The team explores opportunities to improve quality and/or efficiency of current processes in order to reduce overall project effectiveness or cost.

- Identify representatives from each team to participate in process discussion related to people, processes, or tools
- Evaluate successes, challenges, and opportunities for improvement
- Assess challenges that impact multiple teams
- Develop an action plan to address challenges and/or areas of improvement

PLAY: Program Dashboard

Description: Program Management collects progress from each team and aggregates data to create a holistic view of the total effort.

Objective: Provide a holistic view of progress, risks, and issues associated with the overall initiative.

Technique: On a regular basis (either weekly, bi-weekly, or each iteration), Project Leads provide a progress update on the status of each team to the Program Lead. Data reported may include the following elements: planned work vs. completed work, requirements volatility, team cycle time, etc.

- Establish key metrics that provide actionable intelligence to executive leadership team
- Determine process for collection and dissemination of program metrics
- Define format and periodicity for distribution of program metrics
- Determine owner for aggregating and delivery of program metrics to key stakeholders

PLAY: Scaling Across Multiple Teams

Description: Multiple teams working together in parallel enhances collaboration and shortens overall timeline.

Objective: Maximize overall efficiency of program team members by doing work in parallel.

Technique: For large initiatives that require multiple workstreams to be managed simultaneously, the organization will benefit from following an integrated approach where Diligence activities and Integration Planning efforts are carried out in parallel. This process enables the project team to share knowledge effectively across workstreams, which shortens the duration of Integration Execution, resulting in shorter overall project duration. By leveraging other plays such as "Multi-team Planning" and "Multi-team Standup," knowledge is disseminated consistently so communication across teams is managed efficiently.

- Consult Agile M&A advisor to define workstreams for program initiative
- Map key processes to each workstream
- Explore efficiency improvement opportunities through the use of work management tool
- Assemble a team for each workstream by identifying required expertise & skillset

PLAY: Clarify Roles & Responsibilities

Description: Teams designate specific roles and responsibilities to ensure clarity in individual areas of accountability.

Objective: Optimize team productivity and effectiveness by ensuring every member of the project understands how to contribute to the overall effort.

Technique: Program Kickoff and consistent reinforcement of team responsibilities will enable collaboration, with focus and maximum performance in mind.

- Define specific project and program-level team roles and areas of responsibility
- Communicate key processes and interaction models for team members
- Explore potential impact to work management tool

PLAY: Project Premortem

Description: Teams roleplay project failure to uncover hidden challenges and strengthen their operational approach.

Objective: Identify potential existential threats to the M&A project by roleplaying project failure.

Technique: Unlike other forms of preliminary risk analysis that attempt to foresee various challenges that could emerge over the project lifecycle, a premortem assumes that the project has already failed and attempts to explain why. By placing the "mortem" examination before, rather than after, the deal, this play allows the deal team to take meaningful steps against project failure, rather than simply reacting after the fact.

- Roleplay failure scenarios to anticipate areas of weakness before the project commences
- Hold Program Retrospectives at a regular cadence
- Work collaboratively to solve problems that have been identified
- Consider how the scenarios (risks and opportunities) you have roleplayed affect your existing plan

PLAY: Fast Learning Cycles

Description: Work is performed in an iterative fashion so that changing priorities and new requests can be managed quickly and efficiently.

Objective: Enable project team to adapt to changing conditions, unexpected requests, and to continue working towards a common objective without delays.

Technique: Implementation of short, iterative cycles enable teams to optimize feedback loops, which contribute to continuous improvement. Consistent application of this play will lead to high-performing teams that are inherently self-learning and achieve consistent results.

- Apply Retrospective collaboration events consistently
- Identify and share key learnings across project teams
- Refine Retrospective process iteratively

PLAY: Decentralize Decision-Making

Description: Teams doing the work is empowered and encouraged to make decisions as needed, and only escalate to leadership team if an impediment requires higher-level authorization.

Objective: Maximize completion of work by empowering the team members closest to the problem to make decisions without the need to engage higher levels of the organizational hierarchy.

Technique: Enabling team members who have the deepest understanding of the situational context to make decisions minimizes the unnecessary handoffs that typically result in delays. In order to apply this play, the management team must provide formal authority and autonomy to the teams.

- Define areas of accountability and authority for various team roles (i.e. contributor role, lead role)

- Encourage efficient decision-making with optimal communication paths for risk management
- Clarify process for escalating high-impact decisions and issues

PLAY: Lightweight Communication Model

Description: Regular touchpoints by teams reduce the need for rigid status meetings and enhance flow of information.

Objective: Minimize the need for recurring status meetings to convey information. Maximize the time spent on performing meaningful, valuable work.

Technique: Hold structured and focused collaboration events for teams on a consistent basis. Escalate critical information on an as-needed basis to executive leadership team.

- Hold Daily Standup for each team
- Hold Program Daily Standups with representatives from each team
- Hold Program Retrospectives on a regular cadence
- Conduct artifact review meeting on a regular cadence
- Re-prioritize new work on a regular cadence
- Manage/distribute project status information automatically via use of tools

Looking for additional guidance on how to implement Agile in your next M&A project?

Free resources are available on **agilema.com** and **dealroom.net**.

- Toolkits
- Guides
- Templates
- Training Videos
- Directory of Advisors

Acknowledgments

I want to sincerely thank all of the industry leaders and innovators who contributed their endless knowledge, feedback, and resources to the creation of this book. Their guidance enabled me to create a truly actionable piece of industry literature. Naturally, our approach to this book was Agile, as we evaluated, tested, and iterated on these theories to a painstaking degree. With that being said, I hope you gain as much from this book as I did in its production.

A special thanks to:

Jake Winchester
Eugene Lai
Alix Jean Vollum
Abigail Hart
Allisha Lopshire
James Harris
Greg Born
Christina Amiry
Chris Hecht
Ben de Haldevang
David Boyd
Toby Tester
Richard Kasperowski

Many of the quotes referenced throughout this book were extracted from M&A Science interviews. M&A Science is an educational podcast I host exploring the intricate world of M&A with industry leaders and practitioners. M&A Science is a great resource for additional thought-leadership, M&A trends, and lessons-learned. The podcast can be found on all major streaming platforms.

About the Author

Kison Patel is the Founder and CEO of DealRoom, a project management solution for complex financial transactions. With a decade of experience as an M&A advisor, Kison devotes his time to realizing and building solutions for more innovative, efficient and people-driven M&A. Through developing technology, educational content and industry training, Kison aims to bring better project management to an industry with growing market pressures, transaction values, and competition.

205 W. Wacker Dr. #617, Chicago IL 60606
800-340-9749 • 312-344-3442 • www.agilema.com

Made in the USA
Las Vegas, NV
29 August 2024

94601780R00085